FRENCH
VISUAL
PHRASE BOOK

LONDON, NEW YORK, MELBOURNE,
MUNICH, DELHI

Senior Editor Angela Wilkes
Art Editor Silke Spingies
Production Editor Lucy Baker
Production Controller Inderjit Bhullar
Managing Editor Julie Oughton
Managing Art Editor Christine Keilty
Reference Publisher Jonathan Metcalf
Art Director Bryn Walls

**Produced for Dorling Kindersley by
SP Creative Design**
Editor Heather Thomas
Designer Rolando Ugolino

Language content for Dorling Kindersley
by First Edition Translations Ltd,
Cambridge, UK
Translator Emmanuelle Rivière
Editor Delphine Clavel
Typesetting Essential Typesetting

First published in Great Britain in 2008
by Dorling Kindersley Limited,
80 Strand, London WC2R 0RL
Penguin Group (UK)

2 4 6 8 10 9 7 5 3 1
001–193216–May/13

A CIP catalogue record for this book is
available from the British Library
ISBN 978-1-4093-3128-5

French Visual Phrase Book is available
as a book on its own, in an audio pack
with a CD, or as part of a complete
language course.

Printed and bound in China by
Leo Paper Products LTD.

Discover more at
www.dk.com

CONTENTS

INTRODUCTION

This book provides all the key words and phrases you are likely to need in everyday situations. It is grouped into themes, and key phrases are broken down into short sections, to help you build a wide variety of sentences. A lot of the vocabulary is illustrated to make it easy to remember, and "You may hear" boxes feature questions you are likely to hear. At the back of the book there is a menu guide, listing about 500 food terms, and a 2,000-word two-way dictionary.

Nouns

All French nouns (words for things, people, and ideas) are masculine or feminine. The gender of singular nouns is usually shown by the word for "the": **le** (masculine) and **la** (feminine). These change to **l'** before a vowel. The plural form is **les**. You can look up the gender of words in the French–English dictionary at the back of the book.

Adjectives

Most French adjectives change endings according to whether they describe a masculine or feminine, singular or plural word. In this book the singular masculine form is shown first, followed by the singular feminine form:

I am lost   **Je suis perdu/perdue**

"You"

There are two ways of saying "you" in French: **vous** (polite form and plural) and **tu** (familiar). In this book we have used **vous**, which is normal with people you don't know.

Verbs

Verbs change according to whether they are in the singular or plural. In phrases where this happens, the singular form of the verb is followed by the plural form:

Where is/are…?   **Où se trouve/trouvent…?**

Pronunciation guide

Below each French word or phrase in this book, you will find a pronunciation guide in italics. Read it as if it were English and you should be understood, but remember that it is only a guide and for the best results you should listen to native speakers and try to mimic them. Some French sounds are different from those in English, so take note of how the letters below are pronounced.

a, à, â	like a in father
au	like o in over
c	before a, o, and u, like k in kite
	before e and i, like s in sun
ç	like s in sun
cc	like cc in accident
ch	like sh in ship
e, eu	like u in puff
è, ê, e	like e in fetch
e, ez, er	like ay in play
g	before a, o, and u, like g in get
	before e, i, and y, like s in leisure
h	silent
i	like ee in feet
j	like s in leisure
o	like o in toll
oi	like wa in wag
ou	like oo in shoot
qu	like k in kite
r	rolled at the back of the throat
u	like ew in dew
ui	like wee in between
w	like v in van

ESSENTIALS

In this section, you will find the essential words and useful phrases you need for basic everyday situations and for getting to know people. Be aware of cultural differences when you are addressing French people, and remember that they tend to be quite formal when greeting each other, using *Monsieur* for men, *Madame* for women and *Mademoiselle* for girls and younger women, and often shaking hands.

GREETINGS

Hello	Bonjour *bohnjoor*
Good evening	Bonsoir *bohnswar*
Good night	Bonne nuit *bonn nwee*
Goodbye	Au revoir *oh ruhvwar*
Hi/bye!	Salut! *sahlew*
Pleased to meet you	Enchanté/Enchantée *ohnshohntay*
How are you?	Comment ça va? *komohn sah vah*
Fine, thanks	Bien, merci *byahn mairsee*
You're welcome	De rien *duh ryahn*
My name is...	Je m'appelle... *juh mahpel*
What's your name?	Vous vous appelez comment? *voo voo zahpuhlay komohn*
What's his/her name?	Comment s'appelle-t-il/elle? *komohn sahpel teel/tel*
This is...	C'est... *say*
Nice to meet you	Au plaisir *oh playzeer*
See you tomorrow	À demain *ah duhmahn*
See you soon	À bientôt *ah byahntoh*

SMALL TALK

Yes/no	Oui/Non *wee/nohn*
Please	S'il vous plaît *seel voo play*
Thank you (very much)	Merci (beaucoup) *mairsee (bohkoo)*
You're welcome	De rien *duh ryahn*
OK/fine	D'accord/Bien *dahkohr/byahn*
Pardon?	Pardon? *pardohn*
Excuse me	Excusez-moi *exkewzay mwa*
Sorry	Désolé/désolée *dayzolay*
I don't know	Je ne sais pas *juh nuh say pah*
I don't understand	Je ne comprends pas *juh nuh kohnprohn pah*
Could you repeat that?	Vous pouvez répéter? *voo poovay raypaytay*
I don't speak French	Je ne parle pas français *juh nuh parl pah frohnsay*
Do you speak English?	Vous parlez anglais? *voo parlay ohnglay*
What is the French for...?	Comment dit-on... en français? *komohn dee tohn... ohn frohnsay*
What's that?	Qu'est-ce que c'est? *kes kuh say*
What's that called?	Ça s'appelle comment? *sah sahpel komohn*
Can you tell me...	Vous pouvez me dire... *voo poovay muh deer*

TALKING ABOUT YOURSELF

I'm from...	Je viens de... *juh vyahn duh*
I'm...	Je suis... *juh swee*
...English	...anglais/anglaise *ohnglay/ohnglaiz*
...American	...américain/américaine *ahmaireekahn/ahmaireeken*
...Canadian	...canadien/canadienne *kanadyahn/kanadyen*
...Australian	...australien/australienne *ohstrahlyahn/ohstrahlyen*
...single	...célibataire *sayleebahtair*
...married	...marié/mariée *maryay*
...divorced	...divorcé/divorcée *deevohrsay*
I am...years old	J'ai...ans *jay...ohn*
I have...	J'ai *jay*
...a boyfriend/girlfriend	...un copain/une copine *uhn kohpahn/ewn kohpeen*

You may hear...

- **D'où venez-vous?**
  doo vuhnay voo
  Where are you from?

- **Vous êtes marié/mariée?**
  voo zayt maryay
  Are you married?

- **Vous avez des enfants?**
  voo zavay day zohnfohn
  Do you have children?

SOCIALIZING

Do you live here?	Vous habitez ici? *voo zahbeetay eesee*
Where do you live?	Vous habitez où? *voo zahbeetay oo*
I am here…	Je suis ici… *juh swee eesee*
…on holiday	…en vacances *ohn vahkohns*
…on business	…pour affaires *poor ahfair*
I'm a student	Je suis étudiant/étudiante *juh swee aytewdyohn/ aytewdyohnt*
I work in…	Je travaille dans… *juh trahvaeey dohn*
I am retired	Je suis retraité/retraitée *juh swee ruhtraytay*
Can I have…	Je peux avoir… *juh puh avwar*
…your telephone number?	…votre numéro de téléphone? *vohtr newmairo duh taylayfon*
…your email address?	…votre adresse email? *vohtr ahdress email*
It doesn't matter	Ce n'est pas grave *suh nay pah grahv*
Cheers	Santé! *sohntay*
Are you alright?	Ça va? *sah vah*
I'm OK	Ça va *sah vah*
What do you think?	Qu'est-ce que vous en pensez ? *kes kuh voo zohn pohnsay*

LIKES AND DISLIKES

I like/love…	J'aime/j'adore… *jaym/jahdohr*
I don't like…	Je n'aime pas… *juh naym pah*
I hate…	Je déteste… *juh daytest*
I quite/really like…	J'aime bien/j'aime beaucoup… *jaym byahn/jaym bohkoo*
Don't you like it?	Vous n'aimez pas ça? *voo naymay pah sah*
I would like…	J'aimerais… *jaymuhray*
I'd like this one/that one	Je voudrais celui-là/celui-ci *juh voodray suhlwee lah/ suhlwee see*
My favourite is…	Mon préféré, c'est… *mohn prayfayray say*
I prefer…	Je préfère… *juh prayfayr*
It's delicious	C'est délicieux *say dayleesyuh*
What would you like to do?	Qu'est-ce que vous voulez faire? *kes kuh voo voolay fair*
I don't mind	Ça m'est égal *sah may taygahl*

You may hear …

- **Vous faites quoi dans la vie?**
  voo fet kwa dohn lah vee
  What do you do?

- **Vous êtes en vacances?**
  voo zayt ohn vahkohns
  Are you on holiday?

- **Vous aimez…?**
  voo zaymay

DAYS OF THE WEEK

What day is it today?	Quel jour sommes-nous aujourd'hui? *kel joor sohm noo ohjoordwee*
Sunday	dimanche *deemohnsh*
Monday	lundi *luhndee*
Tuesday	mardi *mardee*
Wednesday	mercredi *maircruhdee*
Thursday	jeudi *juhdee*
Friday	vendredi *vohndruhdee*
Saturday	samedi *samdee*
today	aujourd'hui *ohjoordwee*
tomorrow	demain *duhmahn*
yesterday	hier *eeyair*
in...days	dans...jours *dohn...joor*

THE SEASONS

le printemps
luh prahntohn
spring

l'été
laytay
summer

MONTHS

January	janvier *johnvyay*
February	février *fayvreeyay*
March	mars *mars*
April	avril *ahvreel*
May	mai *may*
June	juin *jwahn*
July	juillet *jweeyay*
August	août *oot*
September	septembre *sayptohnbr*
October	octobre *ohktohbr*
November	novembre *nohvohnbr*
December	décembre *daysohnbr*

l'automne
lohtonn
autumn

l'hiver
leevair
winter

TELLING THE TIME

What time is it?	Quelle heure est-il? *kel uhr ay teel*
It's nine o'clock	Il est neuf heures *eel ay nuhvuhr*
...in the morning	...du matin *dew mahtahn*
...in the afternoon	...de l'après-midi *duh lahpray meedee*
...in the evening	...du soir *dew swar*

une heure
ewn uhr
one o'clock

une heure dix
ewn uhr dees
ten past one

une heure et quart
ewn uhr ay kar
quarter past one

une heure vingt
ewn uhr vahn
twenty past one

une heure et demie
ewn uhr ay duhmee
half past one

deux heures moins le quart
duh zuhr mwahn luh kar
quarter to two

deux heures moins dix
duh zuhr mwahn dees
ten to two

deux heures
duhzuhr
two o'clock

It's midday/midnight	Il est midi/minuit *eel ay meedee/meenwee*
second	la seconde *lah suhgohnd*
minute	la minute *lah meenewt*
hour	l'heure *luhr*
a quarter of an hour	un quart d'heure *uhn kar duhr*
half an hour	une demi-heure *ewn duhmee uhr*
three-quarters of an hour	trois quarts d'heure *trwa kar duhr*
late	tard *tar*
early	tôt *toh*
soon	bientôt *byahntoh*
What time does it start?	À quelle heure ça commence? *ah kel uhr sah komohns*
What time does it finish?	À quelle heure ça finit? *ah kel uhr sah feenee*

You may hear ...

- À plus tard.
  ah plew tar
  See you later.

- Vous êtes en avance.
  voo zayt ohn nahvohns
  You're early.

- Vous êtes en retard.
  voo zayt ohn ruhtar
  You're late.

THE WEATHER

What's the weather like?	Quel temps fait-il? *kel tohn fayteel*
It's...	Il fait... *eel fay*
...good	...beau *boh*
...bad	...mauvais *mohvay*
...warm	...bon *bohn*
...hot	...chaud *shoh*
...cold	...froid *frwa*
...humid	...humide *ewmeed*

Il y a du soleil
eeleeya du sohlay
It's sunny

Il pleut
eel pluh
It's raining

Il y a des nuages
eeleeya day newahj
It's cloudy

C'est la tempête
say lah tohnpet
It's stormy

What's the forecast?	Quelles sont les prévisions météo? *kel sohn lay prayveezyohn maytayoh*
What's the temperature?	Quelle température fait-il? *kel tohnpayrahtewr fayteel*
It's...degrees	Il fait...degrés *eel fay...duhgray*
It's a beautiful day	C'est une belle journée *say tewn bel joornay*
The weather's changing	Le temps change *luh tohn shohnj*
Is it going to get colder/ hotter?	Il va faire plus froid/chaud? *eel vah fair plew frwa/shoh*
It's cooling down	Le temps se rafraîchit *luh tohn suh rahfrayshee*
Is it going to freeze?	Il va geler? *eel vah juhlay*

Il neige
eel nayj
It's snowing

Il gèle
eel jayl
It's icy

Il y a du brouillard
eeleeya dew brooyar
It's misty

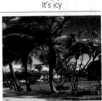

Il y a du vent
eeleeya dew vohn
It's windy

GETTING AROUND

France has an excellent road and motorway system if you are travelling around the country by car. French trains are fast and punctual, linking the main towns and cities, while in the countryside buses connect most mainline railway stations with towns and villages not served by trains. You can also travel by taxi, tram, plane or, in some cities, the *Métro* (underground railway).

ASKING WHERE THINGS ARE

Excuse me, please	Excusez-moi, s'il vous plaît *ekewzay mwa seel voo play*
Where is…	Où se trouve… *oo suh troov*
…the town centre?	…le centre-ville? *luh sohntruh veel*
…the railway station?	…la gare? *lah gar*
…a cash machine?	…un distributeur? *uhn deestreebewtuhr*
How do I get to…?	Pour aller à…? *poor allay ah*
I'm going to…	Je vais… *juh vay*
I'm looking for…	Je cherche… *juh shayrsh*
I'm lost	Je suis perdu/perdue *juh swee payrdew*
Is it near?	C'est près d'ici? *say pray deesee*
Is there a…nearby?	Y a-t-il un…près d'ici? *yateel uhn…pray deesee*
Is it far?	C'est loin ? *say lwahn*
How far is…	À quelle distance se trouve… *a kel deestohns suh troov*
…the town hall?	…la mairie? *lah mairee*
…the market?	…le marché ? *luh marshay*
Can I walk there?	On peut y aller à pied? *ohn puh ee allay ah peeyay*
Do I have to drive?	Il faut prendre la voiture? *eel foh prohndruh lah vwatewr*

CAR RENTAL

Where is the car rental desk?	Où se trouve l'agence de location de voitures? *oo suh troov lajohns duh lokahsyohn duh vwatewr*
I want to hire...	Je voudrais louer... *juh voodray looay*
...a car	... une voiture *ewn vwatewr*
...a motorbike	... une moto *ewn moto*

la berline
lah bairleen
saloon car

le coupé
luh coopay
hatchback

la moto
lah moto
motorbike

le scooter
luh scooter
scooter

le VTT
luh vaytaytay
mountain bike

le vélo de ville
luh vaylo duh veel
road bike

...a bicycle	...un vélo *uhn vaylo*
for...days	pour...jours *poor...joor*

for the weekend	pour le week-end *poor luh weekend*
I'd like...	Je voudrais... *juh voodray*
...an automatic	...une automatique *ewn automateek*
...a manual	...une manuelle *ewn manewayl*
Has it got air conditioning?	Il y a la climatisation? *eeleeya lah cleemateezasyohn*
Should I return it with a full tank?	Je dois la rendre avec le plein d'essence? *juh dwa lah rohndr avek luh plahn daysohns*
Here's my driving licence	Voici mon permis *vwassee mohn pairmee*
Can I hire a...	Je peux louer un... *juh puh looay uhn*
Do you have a...	Vous avez... *voozavay*

le siège enfant
luh siayj ohnfohn
child seat

le casque de vélo
luh kask duh vaylo
cycling helmet

l'antivol
lohnteevol
lock

la pompe
lah pohnp
pump

DRIVING

Is this the road to...?	Cette route mène-t-elle à...? *set root mayn tayl ah*
Where is...	Où se trouve.:. *oo suh troov*
...the nearest garage?	...le garage le plus proche? *luh garaj luh plew prosh*
I'd like...	Je voudrais... *juh voodray*
...some petrol	...de l'essence *duh laysohns*
...40 litres of unleaded	...40 litres de sans plomb *kahrohnt leetruh duh sohn plohn*
...30 litres of diesel	...30 litres de diésel *trohnt leetruh duh dyayzayl*
Fill it up, please	Le plein, s'il vous plaît *luh plahn, seel voo play*
Where do I pay?	Je paye où? *juh payuh oo*
The pump number is...	Le numéro de la pompe est le... *luh newmairo duh lah pohnp ay luh*
Can I pay by credit card?	Je peux payer par carte bancaire? *juh puh payay par cart bohnkair*

la station-service
lah stahsyohn sairvees
Petrol station

Please can you check...	Vous pouvez vérifier... *voo poovay vayreefyay*
...the oil	...le niveau d'huile *luh neevoh dweel*
...the tyre pressure	...la pression des pneus *lah praysyon day pnuh*

PARKING

Is there a car park nearby?	Y a-t-il un parking près d'ici? *yateel uhn parking pray deesee*
Can I park here?	Je peux me garer ici? *juh puh muh garay eesee*
Is it free?	C'est gratuit? *say gratwee*
How much does it cost?	Ça coûte combien? *sa koot kombyahn*
How much is it...	C'est combien... *say kombyahn*
...per hour?	...par heure? *par uhr*
...per day?	...par jour? *par joor*
...overnight?	....pour une nuit? *poor ewn nwee*

la galerie
lah galree
roofrack

le siège enfant
luh siayj ohnfohn
child seat

THE CAR

le coffre
luh kohfruh
boot

le pot d'échappement
luh poh dayshapmohn
exhaust

la roue
lah roo
wheel

la portière
lah portyair
door

INSIDE THE CAR

l'appuie-tête
lapwee tayt
head rest

la poignée
lah pwanyay
handle

la serrure
lah sairewr
door lock

la ceinture de sécurité
lah sahntewr duh saykewreetay
seat belt

le siège avant
luh siayj avohn
front seat

le pare-brise
luh par breez
windscreen

le capot
luh kapo
bonnet

le phare
luh far
headlight

le pneu
luh pnuh
tyre

le moteur
luh motuhr
engine

le pare-choc
luh par shok
bumper

THE CONTROLS

l'airbag
lairbag
airbag

les feux de détresse
lay fuh duh daytrays
hazard lights

le tableau de bord
luh tabloh duh bohr
dashboard

le volant
luh volohn
steering wheel

le compteur de vitesse
luh kohntuhr duh veetess
speedometer

le klaxon
luh klaxon
horn

la radio
lah rahdyoh
car stereo

le levier de vitesses
luh luhvyay duh veetess
gear stick

le chauffage
luh shofaj
heater

ROAD SIGNS

sens unique
sohns ewneek
one way

rond-point
rohn pwuhn
roundabout

cédez le passage
sayday luh passaj
give way

route prioritaire
root preeyoreetair
priority road

sens interdit
sohns ihntairdee
no entry

défense de stationner
dayfohns duh stasyonay
no parking

limitation de vitesse
leemeetasyohn duh veetess
speed limit

défense de s'arrêter
dayfohns duh saraytay
no stopping

danger
dohnjay
hazard

ON THE ROAD

l'horodateur
lohrodatuhr
parking meter

les feux
lay fuh
traffic light

l'agent de la circulation
lajohn duh lah seerkewlasyohn
traffic policeman

la carte
lah kart
map

le passage piéton
luh pasaj pyaytohn
pedestrian crossing

le téléphone d'urgence
luh taylayfon dewrjohns
emergency phone

la place de parking réservée aux handicapés
lah plas duh parking rayzairvay ozohndeekapay
disabled parking

l'autoroute
lotoroot
motorway

la voie d'accès
lah vwa daksay
sliproad

AT THE STATION

Where can I buy a ticket?	Où peut-on acheter des billets? *oo puh tohn ashuhtay day beeyay*
Is there an automatic ticket machine?	Y a-t-il un guichet automatique? *yateel uhn geeshay automateek*

le guichet automatique
luh geeshay automateek
automatic ticket machine

le billet
luh beeyay
ticket

How much is a ticket to…?	Combien coûte un billet pour…? *kombyahn koot uhn beeyay poor*
Two tickets to…	Deux billets pour… *duh beeyay poor*
I'd like…	Je voudrais… *juh voodray*
…a single ticket to…	…un aller simple pour… *uhn allay sahnpl poor*
…a return ticket to…	…un aller-retour pour… *uhn allay ruhtoor poor*
…a first class ticket	…un billet première classe *uhn beeyay pruhmyair class*
…a standard class ticket	…un billet deuxième classe *uhn beeyay duhzyaym class*
I'd like to…	Je voudrais… *juh voodray*
…reserve a seat	…réserver une place *rayzairvay ewn plass*

...on the TGV to...	...dans le TGV pour... *dohn luh tayjayvay poor*
...book a couchette	...réserver une couchette *rayzairvay ewn kooshet*
Is there a reduction...?	Il y a une réduction...? *eeleeya ewn raydewksyohn*
...for children?	...pour les enfants? *poor layzohnfohn*
...for students?	...pour les étudiants? *poor layzaytewdyohn*
...for senior citizens?	...pour les personnes âgées? *poor lay pairson zahjay*
Is there a restaurant car?	Y a-t-il un wagon-restaurant? *eeyateel uhn vahgon raystohrohn*
Is it a fast/slow train?	C'est un train rapide/lent? *say uhn trahn rapeed/lohn*
Is it a high-speed train?	C'est un train à grande vitesse ? *say uhn trahn ah grand veetess*
Do I stamp the ticket before boarding?	Il faut composter avant de prendre le train? *eel fo kohnpostay ahvohn duh prohndruh luh trahn*

You may hear...

• Le train partira de la voie...
luh trahn parteera duh lah vwa
The train leaves from platform...

• Il faut changer de train.
eel fo shohnjay duh trahn
You must change trains.

TRAVELLING BY TRAIN

Do you have a timetable?	Vous avez les horaires? *voozavay layzorair*
What time is...	À quelle heure est... *ah kel uhr ay*
...the next train to...?	... le prochain train pour...? *luh proshahn trahn poor*
...the last train to...?	... le dernier train pour...? *luh dairnyay trahn poor*
Which platform does it leave from?	De quelle voie part-il? *duh kel vwa parteel*
What time does it arrive in...?	À quelle heure arrive-t-il à...? *akel uhr areevteel ah*
How long does it take?	Combien de temps dure le voyage? *kombyahn duh tohn dewr luh vwayaj*
Is this the train for...?	C'est le train pour...? *say luh trahn poor*
Is this the right platform for...?	C'est le bon quai pour...? *say luh bohn kay poor*
Where is platform three?	Le quai numéro trois, s'il vous plaît? *luh kay newmairo trwa, seel voo play*
Does this train stop at...?	Ce train s'arrête à...? *suh trahn sarayt ah*

You may hear...

- Il faut composter son billet.
  eel foh kohnpostay sohn beeyay
  You must validate your ticket.

- Utilisez la borne orange.
  ewteeleezay lah born orohnj
  Use the orange machine.

Where do I change for…?	Je dois changer où pour…? *juh dwa shohnjay oo poor*
Is this seat free?	Cette place est libre? *set plass eh libruh*
I've reserved this seat	J'ai une réservation pour cette place *jay ewn rayzairvasyohn poor set plass*
Do I get off here?	Je descends ici? *juh daysohn eesee*
Where is the underground station?	Où se trouve la station de métro? *oo suh troov lah stahsyohn duh maytroh*
Which line goes to…?	Quelle est la ligne pour…? *kel ay lah leenyuh poor*
How many stops is it?	C'est dans combien d'arrêts? *say dohn kombyahn daray*

le hall de gare
luh ohl duh gar
concourse

le train
luh trahn
train

le wagon-restaurant
luh vagohn raystohrohn
dining car

la couchette
lah kooshet
couchette

BUSES

When is the next bus to…?	À quelle heure est le prochain bus pour…? *ah kel uhr ay luh proshahn bews poor*
What is the fare to…?	Combien coûte le ticket pour…? *kombyahn koot luh teekay poor*
Where is the bus stop?	Où se trouve l'arrêt de bus? *oo suh troov laray duh bews*
Is this the bus stop for…	C'est le bus pour… *say le bews poor*
Does the number 4 stop here?	Le quatre s'arrête ici? *luh katr sarayt eesee*
Where can I buy a ticket?	Où peut-on acheter des tickets? *oo puh tohn ashuhtay day teekay*
Can I pay on the bus?	Je peux payer dans le bus? *juh puh payay dohn luh bews*
Which buses go to the city centre?	Quels bus vont au centre ville? *kel bews vohnt oh sohntruh veel*
Will you tell me when to get off?	Vous m'indiquerez quand descendre? *voo mahndeekeray kohn daysohndruh*
I want to get off!	Je veux descendre! *juh vuh daysohndruh*

le bus
luh bews
bus

la gare routière
lah gar rootyair
bus station

TAXIS

Where can I get a taxi?	Où peut-on trouver un taxi? *oo puh tohn troovay uhn taxi*
Can I order a taxi?	Je peux commander un taxi? *juh puh komohnday uhn taxi*
I want a taxi to…	Je voudrais un taxi pour aller à… *juh voodray uhn taxi poor allay ah*
Can you take me to…	Pouvez-vous m'emmener à… *poovay voo mohnmuhnay ah*
Is it far?	C'est loin? *say lwahn*
How much will it cost?	Quel sera le prix de la course? *kel suhrah luh pree duh la koors*
Can you drop me here?	Vous pouvez me laisser là? *voo poovay muh laysay la*
What do I owe you?	Je vous dois combien? *juh voo dwa kombyahn*
Keep the change	Gardez la monnaie *garday lah monay*
Can I have a receipt?	Je peux avoir un reçu? *juh puh awvar uhn ruhsew*
Please wait for me	Attendez-moi *atohnday mwa*

le taxi
luh taxi
taxi

la borne de taxis
lah born duh taxi
taxi rank

BOATS

Are there any boat trips?	Y a-t-il des balades en bateau? *eeyateel day balad ohn bato*
Where does the boat leave from?	D'où part le bateau? *doo par luh bato*
When is...	À quelle heure part... *a kel uhr par*
...the next boat to...?	...le prochain bateau... *luh proshahn bato poor*
...the first boat?	... le premier bateau? *luh pruhmyay bato*
...the last boat?	... le dernier bateau? *luh dairnyay bato*
I'd like two tickets for...	Je voudrais deux billets pour... *juh voodray duh beeyay poor*
...the cruise	la croisière *lah krwazyair*

le ferry
luh ferry
ferry

l'hydroglisseur
leedrogleessuhr
hydrofoil

le yacht
luh yaht
yacht

l'aéroglisseur
lahairogleessuhr
hovercraft

...the river trip	...la balade en rivière *lah balad ohn reevyair*
How much is it for...	C'est combien pour... *say kombyahn poor*
...a car?	...une voiture? *ewn vwatewr*
...a family?	...une famille? *ewn fameey*
...a cabin?	...une cabine? *ewn kahbeen*
Can I buy a ticket on board?	On peut acheter les billets une fois sur le bateau? *ohn puh ashuhtay leh beeyay ewn fwa sewr luh bato*
Is there wheelchair access?	Il y a un accès handicapés? *eeleeya uhn aksay ohndeekapay*

le gilet de sauvetage
luh jeelay duh sovtaj
life jacket

la bouée de sauvetage
lah booay duh sovtaj
lifebuoy

le catamaran
luh catamarohn
catamaran

le bateau de plaisance
luh bato duh playzohns
pleasure boat

AIR TRAVEL

Which terminal do I need?	Je vais à quel terminal? *juh vay ah kel tairmeenal*
Where do I check in?	Où se trouve l'enregistrement? *oo suh troov lohnruhjeestruhmohn*
Where is/are...	Où se trouve/trouvent... *oo suh troov*
...the arrivals hall?	...les arrivées? *lay zareevay*
...the departures hall?	...les départs? *lay daypar*
...the boarding gate?	...l'embarquement? *lohnbarkuhmohn*
I'm travelling...	Je voyage... *juh vwayaj*
...economy	...en classe économique *ohn class aykonomik*
...business class	...en classe affaires *ohn class ahfair*
Here is my...	Voici mon/ma/mes... *vwassee mohn/mah/may*

le sac fourre-tout
luh sac foor too
holdall

le repas servi à bord
luh ruhpah sairvee ah bohr
flight meal

le passeport
luh passpor
passport

la carte d'embarquement
lah kart dohnbarkuhmohn
boarding pass

I'm checking in one suitcase	J'ai une valise à enregistrer *jay ewn valeez ah ohnruhjeestray*
I packed it myself	J'ai fait mes bagages moi-même *jay fay may bagaj mwa maym*
I have one piece of hand luggage	J'ai un bagage à main *jay uhn bagaj ah mahn*
What is the weight allowance?	Quel est le poids maximum autorisé? *kel ay luh pwa mahkseemuhm ohtohreezay*
How much is excess baggage?	Combien coûte le surplus de bagage? *kombyahn koot luh sewrplew duh bagaj*
Will a meal be served?	Un repas est servi dans l'avion? *uhn ruhpah ay sairvee dohn lahvyohn*
I'd like…	Je voudrais… *juh voodray*
…a window seat	…une place fenêtre *ewn plass fuhnaytr*
…an aisle seat	…une place couloir *ewn plass koolwar*

You may hear …

- **Votre passeport/billet s'il vous plaît.**
  votruh passpor/beeyay seel voo play
  Your passport/ticket please.

- **C'est votre sac?**
  say votruh sack
  Is this your bag?

AT THE AIRPORT

Here's my...	Voici... *vwassee*
...boarding pass	...ma carte d'embarquement *ma kart dohnbarkuhmohn*
...passport	...mon passeport *mohn passpor*
Can I change some money?	Je peux faire du change? *juh puh fair dew shohnj*

le chèque de voyage
luh shayk duh vwayaj
traveller's cheque

le contrôle des passeports
luh kohntrol day passpor
passport control

What is the exchange rate?	Quel est le taux de change? *kel ay luh toduh shohnj*
Is the flight to...on time?	Le vol pour...est à l'heure? *luh vol poor...ayt a luhr*
Is the flight delayed?	Le vol est en retard? *luh vol ayt ohn ruhtar*
How late is it?	Le vol est en retard de combien de temps? *luh vol ayt onh ruhtar duh kombyahn duh tohn*
Which gate does flight... leave from?	Le vol numéro...part de quelle porte d'embarquement? *luh vol newmairo...par duh kel portuh dohnbarkuhmohn*
What time do I board?	À quelle heure est l'embarquement? *a kel uhr ay lohnbarkuhmohn*

Where are the trolleys?	Où sont les chariots? *oo sohn lay shareeo*
Here is the reclaim tag	Voici le ticket *vwassee luh teekay*
I can't find my baggage	Je ne trouve pas mes bagages *juh nuh troov pa may bagaj*

le magasin hors taxe
luh magazahn or tax
duty-free shop

le pilote
luh peelot
pilot

l'hôtesse de l'air
lotess duh lair
air stewardess

l'avion
lavyohn
aeroplane

le enregistrement
luh ohnruhjeestruhmohn
check-in

le retrait des bagages
luh ruhtray day bagaj
baggage reclaim

EATING OUT

It is not difficult to eat well and inexpensively in France. You can choose from cafés and bars, which serve a variety of drinks and snacks, *bistros* (small bars which are often family-run and serve local and traditional dishes) and *brasseries*, which are usually larger and noisier. If you want a gastronomic meal in more formal surroundings, you can eat at a more expensive restaurant but you may have to book in advance.

MAKING A RESERVATION

I'd like to book a table...	Je voudrais réserver une table... *juh voodray rayzairvay ewn tabluh*
...for lunch/dinner	...pour déjeuner/dîner *poor dayjuhnay/deenay*
...for four people	...pour quatre personnes *poor katruh pairson*
...for this evening at seven	...pour ce soir à sept heures *poor suh swar a set uhr*
...for tomorrow at one	...pour demain à une heure *poor duhmahn a ewn uhr*
...for lunchtime today	...pour déjeuner, aujourd'hui *poor dayjuhnay ohjoordwee*
Do you have a table earlier/later?	Vous avez une table un peu plus tôt/tard? *voo zavay ewn tabluh uhn puh plew toh/tar*
My name is...	Je m'appelle... *juh mapel*
My telephone number is...	Mon numéro de téléphone est le... *mohn newmairo duh taylayfon ay luh*
I have a reservation	J'ai réservé *jay rayzairvay*
in the name of...	au nom de... *o nohn duh*
We haven't booked	Nous n'avons pas réservé *noo navohn pa rayzairvay*
Can we sit here?	On peut s'asseoir ici? *ohn puh sasswar eesee*
Can we sit outside?	On peut s'asseoir dehors? *ohn puh sasswar duhor*
I'm waiting for someone	J'attends quelqu'un *jatohn kaylkuhn*

ORDERING A MEAL

Can we see the menu?	La carte, s'il vous plaît? *lah kart seel voo play*
...the wine list?	La carte des vins, s'il vous plaît? *lah kart day vahn seel voo play*
Do you have...	Vous avez... *voo zavay*
...a set menu?	...un menu ? *uhn muhnew*
...a fixed-price menu?	...un menu du jour? *uhn muhnew dew joor*
...a children's menu?	...un menu pour enfants? *uhn muhnew poor ohnfohn*
...an à la carte menu	...une carte? *ewn kart*
What are today's specials?	Il y a des plats du jour? *eeleeya day plah dew joor*
What do you recommend?	Qu'est-ce-que vous recommandez? *kes kuh voo ruhkomohnday*
What is this?	Qu'est-ce que c'est? *kes kuh say*

You may hear...

- **Vous avez réservé?**
  voo zavay rayzairvay
  Do you have a reservation?

- **À quel nom?**
  ah kel nohn
  In what name?

- **Asseyez-vous.**
  ahsayay voo
  Please be seated.

- **Vous avez choisi?**
  voo zavay shwazee
  Are you ready to order?

Are there any vegetarian dishes?	Vous avez des plats végétariens?
	voo zavay deh plah vayjaytahryahn
I can't eat...	Je suis allergique...
	juh swee ahlairjeek
...dairy foods	...aux produits laitiers
	oh prohdwee laytyay
...nuts	...aux noix
	oh nwa
...wheat	...au blé
	oh blay
To start, I'll have...	En entrée, je vais prendre...
	ohn ohntray juh vay prohndr
Can we have...	On peut avoir...
	ohn puh avwar
...some water	...de l'eau?
	duh loh
...some bread?	...du pain?
	dew pahn
...the dessert menu?	...la carte des desserts?
	lah kart day dayssair

Reading the menu

• **Entrées** *ohntray*	Starters
• **Hors-d'œuvre** *ohr duhvr*	First courses
• **Plats principaux** *plah prahnseepoh*	Main courses
• **Légumes** *laygewm*	Vegetables
• **Fromages** *frohmaj*	Cheeses
• **Desserts** *dayssair*	Desserts

COMPLAINING

I didn't order this	Je n'ai pas commandé ça *juh nay pah kornohnday sa*
You forgot my dessert	Vous avez oublié mon dessert *voozavay oobleeyay mohn dayssair*
I can't wait any longer	Je ne peux plus attendre *juh nuh puh plews atohndru*

PAYING

That was delicious	C'était délicieux *saytay dayleessyuh*
The bill, please	L'addition, s'il vous plaît *ladeesyohn seel voo play*
Can I have...	Je peux avoir... *juh puh avwar*
...a receipt?	...un reçu? *uhn ruhssew*
...an itemized bill?	...les détails de l'addition? *lay daytaeey duh ladeesyohn*
Is service included?	Le service est compris? *luh sairvees ay kohnpree*
There's a mistake here	Il y a une erreur ici *eeleeyah ewn airuhr eesee*

You may hear...

- Nous n'acceptons pas les cartes de crédit.
  noo nakseptohn pah lay kart duh kraydee
  We don't take credit cards.

- Tapez votre code secret.
  tapay votruh kohd suhkray
  Please enter your PIN.

CROCKERY AND CUTLERY

la petite assiette
lah puhteet assyet
side plate

le bol
luh bohl
bowl

le sel
luh sayl
salt

le poivre
luh pwahvruh
pepper

la tasse et la soucoupe
lah tass ay lah sookoop
cup and saucer

le verre
luh vair
glass

la cuiller à café
la kweeyair ah kafay
teaspoon

la cuiller à dessert
lah kweeyair ah dayssair
dessertspoon

le couteau
luh kooto
knife

la serviette
lah sairvyet
napkin

la fourchette
lah foorshet
fork

l'assiette
lassyet
dinner plate

AT THE CAFÉ OR BAR

The menu, please	Le menu, s'il vous plaît
luh muhnew seel voo play
Do you have…?	Vous avez…?
voozavay
What fruit juices do you have?	Quels jus de fruits avez-vous?
kel jew duh frwee avayvoo
I'd like…	Je voudrais…
juh voodray
I'll have…	Je vais prendre…
juh vay prohndruh

un café au lait
uhn kafay o lay
coffee with milk

un café noir
uhn kafay nwar
black coffee

un expresso
uhn expresso
espresso

un cappuccino
uhn kapoocheeno
cappuccino

You may hear…

- **Vous désirez?**
voo dayzeeray
What would you like?

- **Autre chose?**
otruh shoz
Anything else?

- **Ça sera tout?**
sa suhra too
Will that be all?

un thé au lait/thé nature
uhn tay o lay/tay natewr
tea with milk/black tea

un thé au citron
uhn tay o seetrohn
tea with lemon

un thé à la menthe
uhn tay a lah mohnt
mint tea

un thé vert
uhn tay vair
green tea

une camomille
ewn kamomeey
camomile tea

un chocolat chaud
uhn shokolah sho
hot chocolate

A bottle of…	Une bouteille de… *ewn bootayeey duh*
A glass of…	Un verre de… *uhn vair duh*
A cup of…	Une tasse de… *ewn tass duh*
With lemon/milk	Avec du citron/du lait *avek dew seetrohn/dew lay*
Another…please	Un/une autre…, s'il vous plaît *uhn/ewn otruh seel voo play*
The same again, please	La même chose, s'il vous plaît *la maym shoz seel voo play*

CAFÉ AND BAR DRINKS

un café frappé
uhn kafay frapay
iced coffee

un jus d'orange
uhn jew dorohnj
orange juice

un jus de pomme
uhn jew duh pom
apple juice

un jus d'ananas
uhn jew danana
pineapple juice

un jus de tomate
uhn jew duh tomaht
tomato juice

un jus de raisin
uhn jew duh rayzahn
grape juice

une limonade
ewn leemonahd
lemonade

une orangeade
ewn orohnjad
orangeade

un coca
unh kokah
cola

un gin tonic
uhn djeen tonic
gin and tonic

une bouteille d'eau minérale
ewn bootayeey do meenairal
bottle of mineral water

une eau pétillante
ewn o payteeyohnt
soda water

une bière
ewn byair
beer

un cidre
uhn seedruh
cider

un verre de vin rouge
uhn vair duh vahn rooj
glass of red wine

du vin blanc
dew vahn blohn
white wine

You may hear...

- **Un demi?**
  uhn duhmee
  A half?

- **En bouteille?**
  ohn bootayee
  Bottled?

- **Plate ou pétillante?**
  plaht oo payteeyohnt
  Still or sparkling?

- **Avec des glaçons?**
  avek day glassohn
  With ice?

BAR SNACKS

un sandwich
uhn sohndweech
sandwich

un croque monsieur
uhn krok muhsyuh
grilled cheese sandwich

des olives
day zoleev
olives

des cacahouètes
day kakaooet
nuts

de la vinaigrette
duh lah veenaygret
dressing

une salade
ewn salad
salad

des galettes
day galet
savoury crêpes

des viennoiseries
day vyaynwazuhree
pastry

une glace
ewn glass
ice cream

de la brioche
duh lah breeosh
brioche

FAST FOOD

Can I have...	Je voudrais... *juh voodray*
...to eat in/take away	...sur place/à emporter *sewr plass/ah ohnportay*
...some ketchup/mustard	...du ketchup/de la moutarde *dew ketchup/duh lah mootard*

un hamburger
uhn ohnbuhrguhr
hamburger

un hamburger au poulet
uhn ohnbuhrguhr oh poolay
chicken burger

un roulé
uhn roolay
wrap

un hot dog
uhn ot dog
hot dog

des brochettes
day broshet
kebab

des frites
day freet
French fries

du poulet frit
dew poolay free
fried chicken

une pizza
ewn pizza
pizza

BREAKFAST

Can I have some...	Je peux avoir... *juh puh avwar*
...milk/sugar	...du lait/du sucre *dew lay/dew sewkr*
...artificial sweetener	...de l'édulcorant *duh laydewlkorohn*
...butter	...du beurre *dew buhr*

un café
uhn kafay
coffee

un thé
uhn tay
tea

un chocolat chaud
uhn shokolah sho
hot chocolate

un jus d'orange
uhn jew dorohnj
orange juice

un jus de pomme
uhn jew duh pom
apple juice

du pain
dew pahn
bread

un petit pain
uhn puhtee pahn
bread roll

de la brioche
duh lah breeosh
brioche

un croissant
uhn krwassohn
croissant

un pain au chocolat
uhn pahn o shokolah
chocolate croissant

de la marmelade
duh lah marmuhlahd
marmalade

du miel
dew myayl
honey

des œufs brouillés
dayzuh brooyay
scrambled eggs

un œuf à la coque
uhn nuhf ah lah kok
boiled egg

un œuf poché
uhn nuhf pohshay
poached egg

du pain perdu
dew pahn pairdew
French toast

des fruits frais
day frwee fray
fresh fruit

un yaourt aux fruits
uhn yaoort oh frwee
fruit yoghurt

FIRST COURSES

une soupe
ewn soop
soup

un consommé
uhn kohnsomay
broth/clear soup

une soupe de poisson
ewn soop duh pwassohn
fish soup

une quiche
ewn keesh
savoury tart

un soufflé
uhn sooflay
soufflé

une omelette
ewn omlet
omelette

une piperade
ewn peepuhrad
piperade

des œufs en cocotte
dayzuh ohn kokot
baked eggs

du saumon fumé
dew sohmohn fewmay
smoked salmon

du jambon cru
dew johnbohn krew
cured ham

une assiette de charcuterie
ewn assyet duh sharkewtree
cold meats

des rillettes
day reeyet
rillettes

des crevettes grillées
day kruhvet greeyay
grilled prawns

des coquilles St Jacques
day kokeey sahn jak
scallops

des escargots
day zayskargo
snails

des moules au vin blanc
day mool oh vahn blohn
mussels in white wine

des tomates farcies
day tomat farsee
stuffed tomato

une salade au chèvre chaud
ewn salad oh shayvr sho
goat's cheese salad

une salade aux épinards
ewn salad ozaypeenar
spinach salad

de l'aïoli
duh layolee
aioli

MAIN COURSES

I would like...	Je voudrais... *juh voodray*
...the lamb	...l'agneau *lanyo*
...the pork	...le porc *luh por*
...the beef	...le bœuf *luh buhf*
...the steak	...le steak *luh stayk*
...the ham	...le jambon *luh johnbohn*
...the veal	...le veau *luh voh*
...the chicken	...le poulet *luh poolay*
...the pheasant	...le faisan *luh fuhzohn*
...the turkey	...la dinde *lah dahnd*
...the duck	...le canard *luh kanar*
...the lobster	...le homard *luh ohmar*
...the salmon	...le saumon *luh somohn*

You may see...

des fruits de mer *day frwee duh mair* seafood

du poisson *dew pwassohn* fish

You may hear...

- **Quelle cuisson, pour le steak?**
  kel kweesohn poor luh stayk
  How do you like your steak?

- **Saignant ou rosé?**
  saynyohn oo rohzay
  Rare or medium rare?

- **Bien cuit?**
  byahn kwee
  Well done?

roasted	rôti/rôtie *rohtee*
baked	au four *oh foor*
grilled	grillé/grillée *greeyay*
fried	frit/frite *free/freet*
steamed	à la vapeur *ah lah vapuhr*
poached	poché/pochée *pohshay*
stewed	à l'étuvée *ah laytewvay*
stuffed	farci/farcie *farsee*

de la volaille
duh lah volaeey
poultry

de la viande
duh lah vyohnd
meat

SALADS AND SIDE DISHES

une salade verte
ewn salad vairt
green salad

une salade mixte
ewn salad meext
mixed salad

purée de pommes de terre
pewray duh pom duh tair
mashed potato

des légumes à la vapeur
day laygewm ah lah vapuhr
steamed vegetables

du riz
dew ree
rice

des pâtes
day paht
pasta

des frites
day freet
chips

du couscous
dew kooskoos
couscous

de la ratatouille
duh lah ratatoowee
ratatouille

un tian provençal
uhn teeyohn prohvohnsal
Provençal vegetables

DESSERTS

une mousse au chocolat
ewn moos oh shokolah
chocolate mousse

une crème caramel
ewn kraym karamayl
crème caramel

une crème brûlée
ewn kraym brewlay
crème brûlée

des crêpes
day krayp
pancakes

un sorbet
uhn sorbay
sorbet

une glace
ewn glass
ice cream

un baba au rhum
uhn baba oh rom
rum baba

un gâteau
uhn gato
cake

une tarte aux fruits
ewn tart oh frwee
fruit tart

une tarte tatin
ewn tart tatahn
apple tart

PLACES TO STAY

France has a wide range of places to stay, depending on your personal preference and budget. These range from elegant *hôtels* and historic *châteaux* to smaller, family-run pensions and B & B-style *chambres d'hôtes*. If you want a self-catering option, you can rent a seaside villa, a *gîte* – a house in the country, or find a campsite to park your caravan or put up your tent.

MAKING A RESERVATION

I'd like...	Je voudrais... *juh voodray*
...to make a reservation	...réserver *rayzairvay*
...a double room	...une chambre pour deux personnes *ewn shohnbr poor duh pairson*
...a twin-bedded room	...une chambre à lits jumeaux *ewn shohnbr ah lee jewmoh*
...a single room	...une chambre individuelle *ewn shohnbr ahndeeveedewel*
...a family room	...une chambre familiale *ewn shohnbr fameelyal*
...a disabled person's room	...une chambre adaptée pour les handicapés *ewn shohnbr adaptay poor lay zohndeekapay*
...with a bath/shower	...avec baignoire/douche *avek baynwar/doosh*
...with a sea view	...avec vue sur la mer *avek vew sewr lah mair*
...for two nights	...pour deux nuits *poor duh nwee*
...for a week	...pour une semaine *poor ewn suhmen*
Is breakfast included?	Le petit-déjeuner est compris? *luh puhtee dayjuhnay ay kohnpree*
How much is it...	C'est combien... *say kombyahn*
...per night?	...par nuit? *par nwee*
...per week?	...par semaine? *par suhmen*

CHECKING IN

I have a reservation in the name of...
J'ai réservé au nom de...
jay rayzairvay oh nohn duh

Do you have...
Vous avez...
voozavay

un porteur
uhn portuhr
a porter

les ascenseurs
lay zasohnsuhr
lifts

le service en chambre
luh sairvees ohn shohnbr
room service

le mini bar
luh meenee bar
mini bar

I'd like...
Je voudrais...
juh voodray

...the keys for room...
...les clés de la chambre...
lay klay duh la shohnbr

...a wake-up call at...
...être réveillé à...
aytr rayvayay ah

What time is...
À quelle heure est...
ah kel uhr ay

...breakfast?
...le petit déjeuner?
luh puhtee dayjuhnay

...dinner?
...le dîner?
luh deenay

IN YOUR ROOM

Do you have…	Vous avez… *voo zavay*
another…	un/une autre… *uhn/ewn otruh*
some more…	d'autres… *dotruh*

des oreillers
day zohrayay
pillows

des couvertures
day koovairtewr
blankets

une ampoule
ewn ohnpool
a light bulb

un adaptateur
uhn ahdahptahtuhr
an adapter

I've lost my key | J'ai perdu ma clé *jay pairdew mah klay*

You may hear…

- **Votre chambre est le numéro…**
votruh shohnbr ay luh newmairo
Your room number is…

- **Voici votre clé.**
wwasee votruh klay
Here is your key.

IN THE HOTEL

The room is…	La chambre est… *lah shohnbr ay*
…too hot	…trop chaude *tro shohd*
…too cold	…trop froide *tro frwad*
The TV doesn't work	La télé ne marche pas *lah taylay nuh marshuh pa*

le thermostat
luh tairmosta
thermostat

le radiateur
luh rahdeeyatuhr
radiator

la chambre individuelle
lah shohnbr ahndeeveedewel
single room

la chambre double
lah shohnbr doobluh
double room

le numéro de chambre
luh newmayro duh shohnbr
room number

la bouilloire
lah booywar
kettle

The window won't open	La fenêtre n'ouvre pas *lah fuhnaytr noovruh pa*
I can't get a line	Je n'arrive pas à téléphoner *juh nareev pah ah taylayfonay*

le cintre
luh sahntr
coat hanger

le téléviseur
luh taylayveezuhr
television

le store
luh stohr
venetian blind

la télécommande
lah taylaykomohnd
remote control

CHECKING OUT

When do I have to vacate the room?	À quelle heure faut-il quitter la chambre? *ah kel uhr foteel keetay lah shohnbr*
Is there a porter to carry my bags?	Y a-t-il un porteur pour mes sacs? *eeyateel uhn portuhr poor may sak*
Can I have the bill please	Je peux avoir la note s'il vous plaît? *juh puh avwar lah noht seel voo play*
Can I pay...	Je peux payer... *juh puh payay*
...by credit card?	...par carte de crédit? *par kart duh kraydee*
...cash?	...en liquide? *ohn leekeed*
I'd like a receipt	Je voudrais un reçu *juh voodray uhn ruhsew*

IN THE BATHROOM

la baignoire
lah baynwar
bathtub

le bidet
luh beeday
bidet

le savon
luh savohn
soap

les serviettes
lay sairvyet
towels

le peignoir
luh paynwar
bathrobe

le bain moussant
luh bahn moosohn
bubblebath

le gel douche
luh jel doosh
shower gel

le déodorant
luh dayodorohn
deodorant

le lait corps
luh lay kohr
body lotion

le dentifrice
luh dohnteefrees
toothpaste

la brosse à dents
lah bros ah dohn
toothbrush

le bain de bouche
luh bahn duh boosh
mouthwash

le rasoir électrique
luh razwar aylayktreek
electric razor

la mousse à raser
lah moos ah razay
shaving foam

le rasoir
luh razwar
razor

le sèche-cheveux
luh saysh shuhvuh
hairdryer

le shampooing
luh shohnpooahn
shampoo

l'après-shampooing
lapray shohnpooahn
conditioner

le coupe-ongles
luh koopohngluh
nail clippers

les ciseaux à ongles
lay seezo ah ohngluh
nail scissors

SELF-CATERING

Can we have...	On peut avoir... *ohn puh avvwar*
...the key, please?	...la clé, s'il vous plaît? *lah klay seel voo play*
...an extra bed?	...un lit supplémentaire? *uhn lee sewplaymohntair*
...a child's bed?	...un lit d'enfant? *uhn lee dohnfohn*

la chaise haute
lah shayz oht
high chair

le lit d'enfant
luh lee dohnfohn
cot

...more cutlery	...d'autres couverts *dotruh koovair*
...more crockery	plus de vaisselle *plew duh vaysel*
Where is...	Où se trouve... *oo suh troov*
...the fusebox?	...la boîte à fusibles? *lah bwat ah fewzeebl*
...the stopcock?	...l'arrivée d'eau? *lareevay do*
...the supermarket?	...le supermarché? *luh sewpairmarshay*
...the nearest shop?	...le magasin le plus proche? *luh magahzahn luh plew prosh*
Do you do babysitting?	Vous gardez les enfants? *voo gahrday lay zohnfohn*
How does the heating work?	Comment marche le chauffage? *kohmohn marsh luh shofaj*

Is there...	Y a-t-il... *eeyateel*
...air conditioning?	...la climatisation? *lah klimateezasyohn*
...central heating?	...le chauffage central? *luh shofaj sohntral*

le ventilateur
luh vohnteelatuhr
fan

le convecteur
luh kohnvektuhr
convector heater

When does the cleaner come?	À quelle heure vient la femme de ménage? *ah kel uhr vyahn lah fahm duh maynaj*
Where do I put the rubbish?	Où faut-il mettre ses déchets? *oo foteel maytruh say dayshay*
Do you take pets?	Vous acceptez les animaux? *voo zaksaytay lay zaneemo*

le chien
luh shyahn
dog

IN THE VILLA OR GÎTE

Is there an inventory?	Il y a un inventaire? *eeleeya uhn ahnvohntair*
Where is this item?	Où se trouve cet objet? *oo suh troov set objay*
I need...	Il me faut... *eel muh fo*
...an adapter	...un adaptateur *uhn ahdahptahtuhr*
...an extension lead	...une rallonge *ewn ralohnj*
...a torch	...une lampe torche *ewn lohnp torsh*
...matches	...des allumettes *day zalewmet*

le micro-ondes
luh meekro-ohnd
microwave

le fer à repasser
luh fair ah ruhpassay
iron

la planche à repasser
lah plohnsh ah ruhpassay
ironing board

la serpillère et le seau
lah sairpeeyair ay luh so
mop and bucket

la pelle et le balai
lah pel ay luh balay
dustpan and brush

le produit de nettoyage
luh prodwee duh netwayaj
detergent

PROBLEM SOLVING

The shower doesn't work	La douche ne marche pas *lah doosh nuh marshuh pa*
The toilet is leaking	Les toilettes fuient *lay twalet fwee*
Can you mend it today?	Vous pouvez faire les réparations aujourd'hui? *voo poovay fair lay rayparasyohn ojoordwee*
There's no...	Il n'y a pas... *eel neeya pa*
...electricity	...d'électricité *daylektreeseetay*
...water	...d'eau *doh*

la machine à laver
lah masheen ah lahvay
washing machine

le réfrigérateur
luh rayfreejayratuhr
fridge

la poubelle
lah poobel
rubbish bin

la serrure et les clés
lah sairewr ay lay klay
lock and key

le détecteur de fumée
luh daytayktuhr duh fewmay
smoke alarm

l'extincteur
lextahnktuhr
fire extinguisher

KITCHEN EQUIPMENT

l'ouvre-boîte
loovruh bwat
can opener

le décapsuleur
luh daykapsewluhr
bottle opener

le tire-bouchon
luh teer booshohn
corkscrew

la planche à découper
lah plohnsh ah daykoopay
chopping board

le couteau de cuisine
luh kooto duh kweezeen
kitchen knife

l'économiseur
laykonomeezuhr
peeler

le fouet
luh fooeh
whisk

la cuiller en bois
lah kweeyair ohn bwa
wooden spoon

la spatule
lah spatewl
spatula

la râpe
lah rap
grater

la passoire
lah paswar
colander

la poêle
lah pwal
frying pan

la casserole
lah kasrohl
saucepan

le gril
luh greel
grill pan

la marmite
lah marmeet
casserole dish

le bol mélangeur
luh bohl maylohnjuhr
mixing bowl

Le mixeur
luh meexuhr
blender

la plaque de cuisson
lah plak duh kweesohn
baking tray

les gants de cuisine
leh gohn duh kweezeen
oven gloves

le tablier
luh tableeyay
apron

CAMPING

Where is the nearest...	Où se trouve le plus proche... *oo suh troov luh plew prosh*
...campsite?	...terrain de camping? *tairahn duh kohnpeeng*
...caravan site?	...terrain pour caravanes? *tairahn poor kahrahvan*
Can we camp here?	On peut camper ici? *ohn puh kohnpay eesee*
Do you have any vacancies?	Il y a de la place? *eeleeya duh lah plass*
What is the charge...	C'est combien... *say kombyahn*
...per night?	...par nuit? *par nwee*
...per week?	...par semaine? *par suhmen*
Does the price include...	Le prix inclut... *luh pree ahnklew*
...electricity?	...l'électricité? *laylektreeseetay*
...hot water?	...l'eau chaude? *lo shohd*
Are showers extra?	Les douches sont en plus? *lay doosh sohn tohn plews*
We want to stay for...	Nous voulons rester... *noo voolohn restay*

la tente
lah tohnt
tent

le tendeur
luh tohnduhr
guy rope

Can I rent...	On peut louer... *ohn puh looay*
...a tent?	...une tente? *ewn tohnt*
...a bicycle?	...des vélos? *day vaylo*
...a barbecue?	...un barbecue? *uhn barbuhkyoo*
Where are...	Où sont... *oo sohn*
...the toilets?	...les toilettes? *lay twalet*
...the dustbins?	...les poubelles? *lay poobel*
Are there...	Il y a... *eeleeya*
...showers?	...des douches? *day doosh*
...laundry facilities?	...une laverie? *ewn lahvree*
Is there...	Il y a... *eeleeya*
...a swimming pool?	...une piscine? *ewn peeseen*
...a shop?	...un magasin? *uhn magazahn*

You may hear...

- **Ne faites pas de feu.**
  nuh fayt pah duh fuh
  Don't light a fire.

- **Ne buvez pas l'eau.**
  nuh bewvay pah lo
  Don't drink the water.

AT THE CAMPSITE

le matelas gonflable
luh matla gohnflabl
air mattress

le sac de couchage
luh sak duh kooshaj
sleeping bag

la bouilloire de camping
lah booywar duh kohnpeeng
camping kettle

le réchaud
luh raysho
camping stove

le panier à pique-nique
luh panyay ah peek neek
picnic hamper

la bouteille thermos
lah bootayeey tairmos
vacuum flask

la glacière
lah glasyair
coolbox

le barbecue
luh barbuhkyoo
barbecue

l'eau en bouteilles
lo ohn bootayeey
bottled water

le seau
luh so
bucket

la lampe torche
lah lohnp torsh
torch

la pelote de fil
lah puhlot duh feel
ball of string

le maillet
luh mayay
mallet

la boussole
lah boosol
compass

le produit contre les insectes
luh prodwee kohntr layzahnsekt
insect repellent

la crème solaire
lah kraym solair
sunscreen

le pansement
luh pohnsmohn
plaster

l'imperméable
lahnpairmayabl
waterproofs

les chaussures de marche
lay shosewr duh marsh
walking boots

le sac à dos
luh sakado
backpack

SHOPPING

As well as department stores, hypermarkets and specialist shops, France has many picturesque open-air markets in town squares and high streets where you can buy food, clothes and even antiques relatively cheaply. Most shops are open between 9.00am and 6.30pm from Tuesday to Saturday. However, many stores and food shops are shut on Mondays, and in small towns and villages they often close for two hours for lunch.

IN THE STORE

I'm looking for...	Je cherche... *juh shairsh*
Do you have...?	Vous avez...? *voo zavay*
I'm just looking	Je regarde *juh ruhgard*
I'm being served	On s'occupe de moi *ohn sokewp duh mwa*
Do you have any more of these?	Vous en avez d'autres? *voo zohn navay dohtr*
How much is this?	C'est combien? *say kombyahn*
Have you anything cheaper?	Vous avez des articles moins chers? *voo zavay day zarteekl mwahn shair*
I'll take this one	Je prends ça *juh prohn sah*
Where can I pay?	Où sont les caisses? *oo sohn lay kess*
I'll pay...	Je paye... *juh payuh*
...in cash	...en liquide *ohn leekeed*
...by credit card	...par carte de crédit *par kart duh kraydee*
Can I have a receipt?	Je peux avoir un reçu? *juh puh avwar uhn ruhsew*
I'd like to exchange this	Je voudrais échanger cet article *juh voodray ayshohnjay set arteekl*

IN THE BANK

I'd like...	Je voudrais... *juh voodray*
...to make a withdrawal	...retirer de l'argent *ruhteeray duh larjohn*
...to pay in some money	...déposer de l'argent *dayposay duh larjohn*
...to change some money	...faire du change *fair dew shohnj*
...into euros	...en euros *ohn nuhro*
...into sterling	...en livres sterling *ohn leevruh stairling*
Here is my passport	Voici mon passeport *vwassee mohn passpor*
My name is...	Je m'appelle... *juh mahpel*
My account number is...	Mon numéro de compte est le... *mohn newmairo duh kohnt ay luh*
My bank details are...	Voici mes coordonnées bancaires... *vwassee may ko-ordonay bohnkair*

le taux de change
luh toh duh shohnj
exchange rate

le chèque de voyage
luh shayk duh vwayaj
travellers' cheque

le passeport
luh passpor
passport

l'argent
larjohn
money

Do I have...	Il faut... *eel fo*
...to key in my PIN?	...entrer son code secret? *ohntray sohn kohd suhkray*
...to sign here?	...signer ici? *seenyay eesee*
Is there a cash machine?	Il y a un distributeur? *eeleeya uhn deestreebewtuhr*
The cash machine has eaten my card	Le distributeur a avalé ma carte *luh deestreebewtuhr a ahvahlay mah kart*
Can I cash a cheque?	Je peux encaisser un chèque? *juh puh ohnkessay uhn shayk*
Has my money arrived yet?	Mon argent est arrivé? *mohn narjohn ayt ahreevay*
When does the bank open/close?	À quelle heure ouvre/ferme la banque ? *ah kel uhr oovr/fairm lah bohnk*

le distributeur
luh deestreebewtuhr
cash machine

le banquier
luh bohnkyay
bank manager

la carte de crédit
lah kart duh kraydee
credit card

le carnet de chèques
luh karnay duh shayk
chequebook

SHOPS

la boulangerie
lah boolohnjree
baker's

le marchand de légumes
luh marshohn duh laygewm
greengrocer's

la charcuterie
lah sharkewtree
delicatessen

la poissonnerie
lah pwassonree
fishmonger

le bureau de tabac
luh bewro duh taba
tobacconist

la boutique
lah booteek
boutique

le disquaire
luh deeskair
record shop

le magasin de meubles
luh magahzahn duh muhbl
furniture shop

la boucherie
lah booshree
butcher's

l'épicerie
laypeesree
grocer's

le supermarché
luh sewpairmarshay
supermarket

la librairie
lah leebrairee
book shop

le magasin de chaussures
luh magahzahn duh shohsewr
shoe shop

le tailleur
luh tayuhr
tailor's

la bijouterie
lah beejootree
jeweller's

la quincaillerie
lah kahnkahyuhree
hardware shop

AT THE MARKET

I would like…	Je voudrais… *juh voodray*
How much is this?	C'est combien? *say kombyahn*
What's the price per kilo?	C'est combien au kilo? *say kombyahn oh keelo*
It's too expensive	C'est trop cher *say tro shair*
That's fine, I'll take it	C'est bon, je le prends *say bohn juh luh prohn*
I'll take two kilos	Deux kilos, s'il vous plaît *duh keelo seel voo play*
A kilo of…	Un kilo de… *uhn keelo duh*
Half a kilo of…	Une livre de… *ewn leevr duh*
A little more, please	Un peu plus, s'il vous plaît *uhn puh plews seel voo play*
May I taste it?	Je peux goûter? *juh puh gootay*
That's very good. I'll take some	C'est très bon. J'en prends *say tray bohn john prohn*
That will be all, thank you	C'est tout, merci *say too mairsee*

You may hear…

- **Vous désirez?**
  voo dayzeeray
  Can I help you?

- **Vous en voulez combien?**
  voo zohn voolay kombyahn
  How much would you like?

IN THE SUPERMARKET

Where is/are...	Où se trouve/trouvent... *oo suh troov/troov*
...the frozen foods	... les surgelés? *leh sewrjuhlay*
...the drinks aisle?	... le rayon des boissons? *luh rayohn day bwasohn*
...the check-out?	... les caisses? *lay kess*

le chariot
luh shahreeyo
trolley

le panier
luh panyay
basket

I'm looking for...	Je cherche... *juh shairsh*
Do you have any more?	Il vous en reste? *eel voo zohn rest*
Is this reduced?	C'est en promotion? *say tohn promosyohn*
Can you help me pack	Vous pouvez m'aider à mettre les articles dans les sacs? *voo poovay mayday ah maytruh layzarteekl dohn lay sak*
Where do I pay?	Je paye où? *juh pay oo*
Shall I key in my PIN?	J'entre mon code secret? *johntruh mohn kod suhkray*
Can I have a bag?	Je peux avoir un sac? *juh puh avwar uhn sak*

FRUIT

une orange
ewn orohnj
orange

un citron
uhn seetrohn
lemon

un citron vert
uhn seetrohn vair
lime

un pamplemousse
uhn pohnpluhmooss
grapefruit

une pêche
ewn paysh
peach

une nectarine
ewn nayktareen
nectarine

un abricot
uhn nabreeko
apricot

une prune
ewn prewn
plum

des cerises
day suhreez
cherries

des myrtilles
day meerteeyuh
blueberries

une fraise
ewn frayz
strawberry

une framboise
ewn frohnbwaz
raspberry

un melon
uhn muhlohn
melon

du raisin
dew rayzahn
grapes

une banane
ewn banan
banana

une grenade
ewn gruhnad
pomegranate

une pomme
ewn pom
apple

une poire
ewn pwar
pear

un ananas
uhn nananas
pineapple

une mangue
ewn mohng
mango

VEGETABLES

une pomme de terre
ewn pom duh tair
potato

des carottes
day karot
carrots

un poivron
uhn pwavrohn
pepper

des piments
day peemohn
chillis

une aubergine
ewn obairjeen
aubergine

une tomate
ewn tomat
tomato

un oignon vert
uhn onyohn vair
spring onion

un poireau
uhn pwaro
leek

un oignon
uhn onyohn
onion

de l'ail
duh laeey
garlic

des champignons
day shohnpeenyohn
mushrooms

une courgette
ewn koorjet
courgette

un concombre
uhn kohnkohnbr
cucumber

des haricots verts
day areeko vair
French beans

des petits pois
day puhtee pwa
garden peas

du céleri
dew saylayree
celery

des épinards
dayzaypeenar
spinach

du brocoli
dew brokolee
broccoli

un chou
uhn shoo
cabbage

une laitue
ewn laytew
lettuce

MEAT AND POULTRY

May I have...
Je peux avoir...
juh puh avwar

...a slice of...?
...une tranche de...?
ewn trohnsh duh

...a piece of...?
...un morceau de...?
uhn morso duh

du jambon
dew johnbohn
ham

de la viande hachée
duh lah vyohnd ashay
mince

un steak
uhn stayk
steak

un filet
uhn feelay
fillet

une côte
ewn kot
chop

un gigot d'agneau
uhn jeego danyo
leg of lamb

du poulet
dew poolay
chicken

du canard
dew kanar
duck

FISH AND SHELLFISH

de la truite
duh lah trweet
trout

du saumon
dew somohn
salmon

du cabillaud
dew kabeeyo
cod

du bar
dew bar
sea bass

de la dorade
duh lah dorad
sea bream

des sardines
day sardeen
sardine

du crabe
dew krab
crab

un homard
uhn omar
lobster

des crevettes
day kruhvet
prawns

des coquilles St Jacques
day kokeey sahn jak
scallops

BREAD AND CAKES

un petit pain
uhn puhtee pahn
roll

une baguette
ewn baget
French stick

du pain au levain
dew pahn oh luhvahn
sourdough bread

de la brioche
duh lah breeosh
brioche

un croissant
uhn krwassohn
croissant

un pain au chocolat
uhn pahn oh shokolah
pain au chocolat

la tarte au citron
lah tart oh seetrohn
lemon tart

un éclair au chocolat
uhn ayclair oh shokolah
chocolate éclair

une tarte aux fruits
ewn tart oh frwee
fruit tart

des madeleines
day madlayn
sponge cakes

DAIRY PRODUCE

du lait entier
dew lay ohntyay
whole milk

du lait demi-écrémé
dew lay duhmee aykraymay
semi-skimmed milk

de la crème liquide
duh lah kraym leekeed
single cream

de la crème fraîche
duh lah kraym fraysh
sour cream

du yaourt
dew yaoort
yoghurt

du beurre
dew buhr
butter

du camembert
dew kamohnbair
camembert

du fromage râpé
dew fromaj rapay
grated cheese

du fromage de chèvre
dew fromaj duh shayvr
goat's cheese

du lait de chèvre
dew lay duh shayvr
goat's milk

NEWSPAPERS AND MAGAZINE

Do you have...	Vous avez... *voo zavay*
...any more postcards?	...d'autres cartes postales? *dohtr kart postal*
...a book of stamps?	...des timbres? *day tahnbr*
...airmail stamps?	...des timbres par avion? *day tahnbr par avyohn*
...a packet of envelopes?	...un paquet d'enveloppes? *uhn pakay dohnvlop*
...some sticky tape?	...du scotch? *dew scotch*

une carte postale
ewn kart postal
postcard

des timbres
day tahnbr
stamps

un crayon
uhn krayohn
pencil

un stylo
uhn steelo
pen

You may hear...

- **Vous avez quel âge ?**
  voo zavay kel aj
  How old are you?

- **Vous avez une carte d'identité ?**
  voo zavay ewn kart deedohnteetay
  Do you have ID?

I'd like…	Je voudrais… *juh voodray*
…a pack of cigarettes	…un paquet de cigarettes *uhn pakay duh seegaret*
…a box of matches	…des allumettes *deh zalewmet*

du tabac
dew taba
tobacco

un briquet
uhn breekay
lighter

des chewing-gums
day shuhweengom
chewing gum

des bonbons
day bohnbohn
sweets

un journal
uhn joornal
newspaper

un magazine
uhn magazeen
magazine

une BD
ewn bayday
comic

des crayons de couleur
day krayohn duh kooluhr
colouring pencils

BUYING CLOTHES

I am looking for...	Je cherche... *juh shairsh*
I am size...	Je suis taille... *juh swee taeey*
Do you have this...	Vous avez celui-là... *voo zavay suhlwee lah*
...in my size?	...ma taille? *ma taeey*
...in small	...le même en S? *luh mem ohn es*
...in medium?	...le même en M? *luh mem ohn em*
...in large?	...le même en L? *luh mem ohn el*
...in other colours?	...d'autres couleurs? *dohtr kooluhr*
Can I try this on?	Je peux essayer? *juh puh aysayay*
Where are the changing rooms?	Où sont les cabines d'essayage? *oo sohn lay kabeen daysayaj*
It's...	C'est... *say*
...too big	...trop grand *troh grohn*
...too small	...trop petit *troh puhtee*
I need...	Il me faut... *eel muh fo*
...a larger size	...la taille au-dessus *lah taeey oh duhsew*
...a smaller size	...la taille en dessous *lah taeey ohn duhsoo*
I'll take this one	Je prends celui-là *juh prohn suhlwee lah*

BUYING SHOES

I take shoe size…	Je suis pointure… *juh swee pwahntewr*
Can I try…	Je peux essayer… *juh puh aysayay*
…this pair?	…cette paire? *set pair*
…those ones in the window?	…celles de la vitrine? *sel duh lah veetreen*
These are…	Elles sont… *el sohn*
…too tight	…trop serrées *troh sairay*
…too big	…trop grandes *troh grohnd*
…too small	…trop petites *troh puhteet*
…uncomfortable	…inconfortables *ahnkohnfortabl*
Is there a bigger size?	Vous avez la pointure au-dessus? *voo zavay lah pwahntewr o duhsew*
…a smaller size?	…la pointure en dessous? *lah pwahntewr ohn duhsoo*

Clothes and shoe sizes guide

Women's clothes sizes

UK	6	8	10	12	14	16	18	20
Europe	34	36	38	40	42	44	46	48
USA	4	6	8	10	12	14	16	18

Men's clothes sizes

UK	36	38	40	42	44	46	48	50
Europe	46	48	50	52	54	56	58	60
USA	36	38	40	42	44	46	48	50

Women's shoes

UK	3	4	5	6	7	8	9
Europe	36	37	38	39	40	42	43
USA	5	6	7	8	9	10	11

CLOTHES AND SHOES

une robe
ewn rob
dress

une robe de soirée
ewn rob duh swaray
evening dress

une veste
ewn vest
jacket

un pull
uhn pewl
jumper

un jean
uhn djeen
jeans

une jupe
ewn jewp
skirt

des chaussures de sport
day shosewr duh spor
trainers

des bottes
day bot
boots

un sac à main
uhn sak a mahn
handbag

une ceinture
ewn sahntewr
belt

le costume
luh kostewm
suit

le manteau
luh mohnto
coat

une chemise
ewn shuhmeez
shirt

un t-shirt
uhn teeshuhrt
t-shirt

un short
uhn short
shorts

des chaussures à talon
day shosewr ah talohn
high-heel shoes

des chaussures de ville
day shosewr duh veel
lace-up shoes

des sandales
day sohndal
sandals

des tongs
day tohng
flip-flops

des chaussettes
day shoset
socks

AT THE GIFT SHOP

I'd like to buy a gift for...	Je cherche un cadeau pour... *juh shairsh uhn kado poor*
...my mother/father	...ma mère/mon père *ma mair/mohn pair*
...my daughter/son	...ma fille/mon fils *ma feeyuh/mohn fees*
...a child	...un enfant *uhn nohnfohn*
...a friend	...un ami/une amie *uhn namee/ewn amee*
Can you recommend something?	Vous pouvez me conseiller quelque chose? *voo poovay muh kohnsayay kelkuh shoz*
Do you have a box for it?	Vous avez une boîte? *voo zavay ewn bwat*
Can you gift-wrap it?	Vous pouvez me faire un paquet-cadeau? *voo poovay muh fair uhn pakay kado*

un collier
uhn kolyay
necklace

un bracelet
uhn brasslay
bracelet

une montre
ewn mohntr
watch

des boutons de manchette
day bootohn duh mohnshet
cufflinks

une poupée
ewn poopay
doll

une peluche
ewn puhlewsh
soft toy

un portefeuille
uhn portuhfuhy
wallet

des chocolats
day shokolah
chocolates

I want a souvenir of…	Je cherche un souvenir de… *juh shairsh uhn soovuhneer duh*
Is there a guarantee?	Il y a une garantie? *eeleeya ewn garohntee*
Can I exchange this?	C'est échangeable en cas de problème? *set ayshohnjabl ohn ka duh problaym*

You may hear...

- **C'est pour offrir ?**
  say poor ofreer
  Is it for a present?

- **Vous voulez un paquet-cadeau?**
  voo voolay uhn pakay kado
  Shall I gift-wrap it?

PHOTOGRAPHY

I'd like this film developed	Je voudrais faire développer cette pellicule *juh voodray fair dayvlohpay sayt payleekewl*
When will it be ready?	Ça sera prêt quand? *sah suhra pray kohn*
Do you have an express service?	Vous avez un service rapide? *voo zavay uhn sairvees rapeed*
I'd like...	Je voudrais... *juh voodray*
...the one-hour service	...le service de développement en une heure *luh servees duh dayvlopmohn ohn ewn uhr*

un appareil photo numérique
uhn naparayeey foto newmaireek
digital camera

une carte mémoire
ewn kart maymwar
memory card

une pellicule
ewn payleekewl
roll of film

un album photo
uhn nalbuhm foto
photo album

un cadre
uhn kadr
photo frame

Do you print digital photos?	Vous imprimez les photos numériques? *voo zahnpreemay lay foto newmaireek*
Can you print from this memory stick?	Vous pouvez imprimer à partir de cette carte? *voo poovay ahnpreemay ah parteer duh sayt kart*

un flash
uhn flash
flash gun

un appareil photo
uhn naparayeey foto
camera

un objectif
uhn nobjaykteef
lens

un étui
uhn naytwee
camera bag

You may hear...

• **Quelle taille préférez-vous?**
kel taeey prayfairay voo
What size prints do you want?

• **Mat ou brillant?**
mat oo breeyohn
Matt or gloss?

• **Vous les voulez quand?**
voo lay voolay kohn
When do you want them?

AT THE POST OFFICE

I'd like…	Je voudrais… *juh voodray*
…three stamps, please	…trois timbres, s'il vous plaît *trwa tahnbr seel voo play*
…to register this letter	…envoyer cette lettre en recommandé *ohnvwayay set laytr ohn ruhkomohnday*
…to send this airmail	…envoyer ça par avion *ohnvwayay sah par avyohn*

une enveloppe
ewn ohnvlop
envelope

des timbres
day tahnbr
stamps

une carte postale
ewn kart postahl
postcard

par avion
par avyohn
airmail

You may hear…

- **Quel est le contenu ?**
  kel ay luh kohntuhnew
  What are the contents?

- **Quelle est sa valeur ?**
  kel ay sah valuhr
  What is their value?

How much is...?	Combien ça coûte pour...?
	kombyahn sah koot poor
...a letter to...	...une lettre pour...
	ewn laytr poor
...a postcard to...	...une carte postale pour...
	ewn kart postal poor
...Great Britain	la Grande-Bretagne
	la grohnd bruhtanyuh

un paquet
uhn pakay
parcel

le coursier
luh koorsyay
courier

la boîte aux lettres
la bwat oh laytr
postbox

le facteur
luh faktuhr
postman

...the United States	...les États-Unis
	lay zayta zewnee
...Canada	...le Canada
	luh kanada
...Australia	...l'Australie
	lohstrahlee
Can I have a receipt?	Je peux avoir un reçu?
	juh puh avwar uhn ruhsew
Where can I post this?	Je poste ça où?
	juh post sah oo

TELEPHONES

Where is the nearest phone box?

Où se trouve la cabine téléphonique la plus proche?
oo suh troov lah kabeen taylayfoneek lah plew prosh

le téléphone sans fil
luh taylayfon sohn feel
cordless phone

le téléphone portable
luh taylayfon portabl
mobile phone

la carte de téléphone
lah kart duh taylayfon
phone card

la cabine téléphonique
lah kabeen taylayfoneek
telephone box

la cabine à pièces
lah kabeen ah pyayss
coin phone

le répondeur
luh raypohnduhr
answering machine

Who's speaking?	Qui est à l'appareil? *kee aytah laparayeey*
Hello, this is...	Allô, c'est... *alo, say*
I'd like to speak to...	Je voudrais parler à... *juh voodray parlay ah*
Can I leave a message?	Je peux laisser un message? *juh puh laysay uhn messaj*

INTERNET

Is there an internet café near here?	Il y a un cybercafé près d'ici? *eeleeya uhn seebairkafay pray deesee*
How much do you charge?	C'est combien? *say kombyahn*
Do you have wireless internet?	Vous avez une connexion wifi? *voo zavay ewn koneksyohn weefee*
Can I check my emails?	Je peux regarder mes e-mails? *juh puh ruhgarday may zeemail*
I need to send an email	Je dois envoyer un e-mail *juh dwa ohnvwayay uhn email*
What's your email address?	Quelle est ton adresse e-mail? *kel ay tohn nadrays email*
My email address is...	Mon adresse e-mail est... *mohn nadrays email ay*
Can I send an email from here?	On peut envoyer des e-mails d'ici? *ohn puh ohnvwayay day zeemail deesee*

l'ordinateur portable
lordeenatuhr portabl
laptop

le clavier
luh klavyay
keyboard

le site web
luh seet web
website

l'e-mail
leemail
email

SIGHTSEEING

In most towns, the tourist information office is near the railway station or town hall and the staff will advise you on interesting local places to visit. Most of the national museums in France close on Tuesdays as well as on public holidays, so it is best to check the opening times before visiting.

AT THE TOURIST OFFICE

Where is the tourist information office?	Où se trouve l'office du tourisme? *oo suh troov lofees dew tooreesm*
Can you recommend...	Vous pouvez nous indiquer... *voo poovay noo zahndeekay*
...a guided tour?	...une visite guidée? *ewn veezeet geeday*
...an excursion?	...une excursion? *ewn exkewrsyohn*
Is there a museum?	Il y a un musée? *eeleeya uhn mewzay*
Is it open to the public?	C'est ouvert au public? *say toovair oh pewbleek*
Is there wheelchair access?	Il y a un accès handicapés? *eeleeya uhn aksay ohndeekapay*
Does it close...	Ça ferme... *sah fairm*
...on Sundays?	...le dimanche? *luh deemohnsh*
...on bank holidays?	...les jours fériés? *lay joor fairyay*
Do you have...	Vous avez... *voo zavay*
...a street map?	...un plan de la ville? *uhn plohn duh lah veel*
...a guide?	...un guide? *uhn geed*
...any leaflets?	...des prospectus? *day prospayktews*
Can you show me on the map?	Vous pouvez me montrer sur le plan? *voo poovay muh mohntray sewr luh plohn*

VISITING PLACES

What time...	À quelle heure... *ah kel uhr*
...do you open?	...ouvrez-vous? *oovray voo*
...do you close?	...fermez-vous? *fairmay voo*
I'd like two entrance tickets	Je voudrais deux entrées *juh voodray duh zohntray*
Two adults, please	Deux adultes, s'il vous plaît *duh zadewlt seel voo play*
A family ticket	Un billet familial *uhn beeyay fameelyal*
How much does it cost?	C'est combien? *say kombyahn*
Are there reductions...	Il y a une réduction... *eeleeya ewn raydewksyohn*
...for children?	... pour les enfants? *poor lay zohnfohn*
...for students?	... pour les étudiants? *poor lay zaytewdyohn*

le plan
luh plohn
street map

l'office du tourisme
lofees dew tooreesm
tourist office

le billet d'entrée
luh beeyay dohntray
entrance ticket

l'accès handicapés
laksay ohndeekapay
wheelchair access

Can I buy a guidebook?	Je peux acheter un guide? *juh puh ashuhtay uhn geed*
Is there...	Il y a... *eeleeya*
...an audio-guide?	...un guide audio? *uhn geed audio*
...a guided tour?	...une visite guidée? *ewn veezeet geeday*
...a lift?	...un ascenseur? *uhn asohnsuhr*
...a café?	...un café? *uhn kafay*
...a bus tour?	...une visite en bus? *ewn veezeet ohn bews*
When is the next tour?	À quelle heure est la prochaine visite? *ah kel uhr ay lah proshayn veezeet*

le bus touristique
luh bews tooreesteek
tour bus

You may hear...

- **Vous avez une carte d'étudiant?**
voo zavay ewn kart daytewdyohn
Do you have a student card?

- **Vous avez quel âge?**
voo zavay kel aj
How old are you?

FINDING YOUR WAY

Excuse me	Excusez-moi *exkewzay mwa*
Can you help me?	Vous pouvez m'aider? *voo poovay mayday*
Is this the way to...?	C'est par là...? *say par lah*
How do I get to...	Pour aller... *poor allay*
...the town centre?	...au centre-ville? *oh sohntruh veel*
...the station?	...à la gare? *ah lah gar*
...the museum?	...au musée? *oh mewzay*
...the art gallery?	...à la galerie d'art? *ah lah galree dar*
Is it far?	C'est loin? *say lwahn*
Is it within walking distance?	On peut y aller à pied? *ohn puh ee allay ah peeyay*
Can you show me on the map?	Vous pouvez me montrer sur le plan? *voo poovay muh mohntray sewr luh plohn*

You may hear...

- **Ce n'est pas loin.**
  suh nay pah lwahn
  It's not far away.

- **C'est à dix minutes.**
  say tah dee meenewt
  It takes ten minutes.

- **Il faut prendre un bus.**
  eel foh prohndr uhn bews
  You need to take a bus.

You may hear...

- **Nous sommes là.**
  noo som lah
  We are here.

- **Continuez tout droit...**
  kohnteeneway too drwa
  Keep straight on...

- **...jusqu'au bout de la rue.**
  jewsko boo duh lah rew
  ...to the end of the street.

- **...jusqu'aux feux.**
  jewsko fuh
  ...to the traffic lights.

- **...jusqu'à la grande place.**
  jewska lah grohnd plas
  ...to the main square.

- **Par ici**
  par eesee
  This way

- **Par là**
  par lah
  That way

- **Tournez à droite à...**
  toornay ah drwat ah
  Turn right at...

- **Tournez à gauche à...**
  toornay ah gohsh ah
  Turn left at...

- **Prenez la première...**
  pruhney lah pruhmyair
  Take the first...

- **...à gauche/à droite**
  ah gohsh/ah drwat
  ...on the left/right

- **C'est devant.**
  say duhvohn
  It's in front of you.

- **C'est derrière.**
  say dairyair
  It's behind you.

- **C'est en face.**
  say tohn fass
  It's opposite you.

- **C'est à côté de...**
  say tah kotay duh
  It's next to...

- **C'est indiqué.**
  say tahndeekay
  It's signposted.

- **C'est par là.**
  say par lah
  It's over there.

PLACES TO VISIT

la mairie
lah mairee
town hall

le pont
luh pohn
bridge

le musée
luh mewzay
museum

la galerie d'art
lah galree dar
art gallery

le monument
luh monewmohn
monument

l'église
laygleez
church

la cathédrale
lah kataydral
cathedral

le village
luh veelaj
village

le parc
luh park
park

le port
luh por
harbour

le phare
luh far
lighthouse

le vignoble
luh veenyobl
vineyard

le château
luh shato
castle

la côte
lah koht
coast

la cascade
lah kaskad
waterfall

les montagnes
lay mohntanyuh
mountains

OUTDOOR ACTIVITIES

Where can we go...	Où peut-on aller... *oo puh tonh allay*
...horse riding?	...faire de l'équitation? *fair duh laykeetasyohn*
...fishing?	...pêcher? *payshay*
...swimming?	...nager? *najay*
...walking?	...en randonnée? *ohn rohndonay*
Can we...	On peut... *ohn puh*
...hire equipment?	...louer le matériel? *looay luh matairyayl*
...have lessons?	...prendre des cours? *prohndr day koor*
How much per hour?	C'est combien par heure? *say kombyahn par uhr*
I'm a beginner	Je suis débutant *juh swee daybewtohn*
I'm quite experienced	J'ai pas mal d'expérience *jay pah mal dekspairyohns*
Where's the amusement park?	Où se trouve le parc d'attraction? *oo suh troov luh park datraksyohn*
Can the children go on all the rides?	Les enfants sont autorisés sur tous les manèges? *lay zohnfohn sohn totoreezay sewr too lay manayj*
Is there a playground?	Il y a une aire de jeux? *eeleeya ewn air duh juh*
Is it safe for children?	La sécurité est assurée pour les enfants? *lah saykewreetay etasewray poor lay zohnfohn*

la fête foraine
lah fet forain
fairground

le parc d'attraction
luh park datraksyohn
theme park

le parc safari
luh park safaree
safari park

le zoo
luh zoh
zoo

l'aire de jeux
lair duh juh
playground

le pique-nique
luh peek neek
picnic

la pêche
lah pesh
fishing

l'équitation
laykeetasyohn
horse riding

SPORTS AND LEISURE

France offers the traveller a wide range of cultural events, entertainments, leisure activities, and sports. The French are proud of their funding for the arts, including music, opera, the theatre, and cinema. Their heritage and culture are very important, and most people take a keen interest in the arts, philosophy, and politics. There is also a wide range of sports facilities, from winter sports, climbing, and hiking in the Alps to watersports around the coast and on inland lakes.

LEISURE TIME

I like...	J'aime... *jaym*
...art and painting	...l'art et la peinture *lar ay lah pahntewr*
...films and cinema	...les films et le cinéma *lay feelm ay luh seenayma*
...the theatre	...le théâtre *luh tayahtr*
...opera	...l'opéra *lopaira*
I prefer...	Je préfère... *juh prayfair*
...reading books	...lire *leer*
...listening to music	...écouter de la musique *aykootay duh lah mewzeek*
...watching sport	...regarder le sport *ruhgarday luh spor*
...playing games	...jouer *jooay*
...going to concerts	... aller à des concerts *allay ah day kohnsair*
...dancing	...danser *dohnsay*
...going clubbing	...sortir en boîte *sorteer ohn bwat*
...going out with friends	...sortir avec des amis *sorteer avek dayzamee*
I don't like...	Je n'aime pas... *juh naym pah*
That bores me	Ça m'ennuie *sah mohnwee*
That doesn't interest me	Ça ne m'intéresse pas *sah nuh mahntairess pah*

AT THE BEACH

Can I hire…	Je peux louer… *juh puh looay*
…a jet ski?	…un jet ski? *uhn jet skee*
…a beach umbrella?	…un parasol? *uhn parasol*
…a surfboard?	…une planche de surf? *ewn plohnsh duh surf*
…a wetsuit?	…une combinaison? *ewn kohnbeenayzohn*

la serviette de plage
lah sairvyet duh plaj
beach towel

le ballon de plage
luh balohn duh plaj
beach ball

le transat
luh trohnzat
deck chair

la chaise longue
lah shayz lohng
sun lounger

You may hear…

- **Baignade interdite**
  baynyad ahntairdeet
  No swimming

- **Plage fermée**
  plaj fairmay
  Beach closed.

- **Courants violents**
  koorohn vyolohn
  Strong currents.

les lunettes de soleil
lay lewnet duh solay
sunglasses

le chapeau de paille
luh shapo duh payeey
sunhat

le bikini
luh beekeenee
bikini

la crème solaire
lah kraym solair
suntan lotion

les palmes
lay palm
flippers

le masque et le tuba
luh mask ay luh tewbah
mask and snorkel

How much does it cost?	Ça coûte combien? *sah koot kohnbyahn*
Can I go water-skiing?	Je peux faire du ski nautique? *juh puh fair dew skee noteek*
Is there a lifeguard?	Il y a un sauveteur? *eeleaya uhn sovtuhr*
Is it safe to...	C'est possible de... *say poseebl duh*
...swim here?	...nager ici? *najay eesee*
...surf here?	...faire du surf ici? *fair dew surf eesee*

AT THE SWIMMING POOL

What time...	À quelle heure...
	ah kayl uhr
...does the pool open?	...ouvre la piscine?
	oovruh lah peeseen
...does the pool close?	...ferme la piscine?
	fairm lah peeseen
Is it...	C'est...
	say
...an indoor pool?	...une piscine couverte?
	ewn peeseen koovairt
...an outdoor pool?	...une piscine découverte?
	ewn peeseen daykoovairt
Is there a children's pool?	Il y a un bassin pour les enfants?
	eeleeya uhn basahn poor layzohnfohn
Where are the changing rooms?	Où sont les vestiaires?
	oo sohn lay vaystyair
Is it safe to dive?	On peut plonger?
	ohn puh plohnjay

le brassard
luh brassar
armband

la planche
lah plohnsh
float

les lunettes
lay lewnet
swimming goggles

le maillot de bain
luh mahyo duh bahn
swimsuit

AT THE GYM

le rameur
luh rahmuhr
rowing machine

le cross trainer
luh kross trainuhr
cross trainer

le stepper
luh stepuhr
step machine

le vélo d'exercice
luh vaylo dekzairsees
exercise bike

Is there a gym?	Il y a une salle de gym? *eeleeya ewn sahl duh jeem*
Is it free for guests?	C'est gratuit pour les résidents? *say gratwee poor lay rayzeedohn*
Do I have to wear trainers?	Il faut porter des chaussures de sport? *eel foh portay day shosewr duh spor*
Do I need an induction session?	Il faut suivre une session de présentation? *eel foh sweevr ewn saysyohn duh prayzohntasyohn*
Do you hold...	Vous proposez... *voo propozay*
...aerobics classes?	...des cours d'aérobic? *day koor da-airohbeek*
...Pilates classes?	...des cours de pilates? *day koor duh peelates*
...yoga classes?	...des cours de yoga? *day koor duh yoga*

BOATING AND SAILING

Can I hire...	Je peux louer... *juh puh looay*
...a dinghy?	...un canot pneumatique? *uhn kanoh pnuhmahteek*
...a windsurfer?	...une planche à voile? *ewn plohnsh ah vwal*
...a canoe?	...un canoë? *uhn kanoay*

un gilet de sauvetage
uhn jeelay duh sovtaj
life jacket

une boussole
ewn boosol
compass

...a rowing boat?	...une barque *ewn bark*
Do you offer sailing lessons?	Vous proposez des cours de voile? *voo propozay day koor duh vwal*
Do you have a mooring?	Vous avez un bassin d'amarrage? *voo zavay uhn basahn dahmaraj*
How much is it for the night?	C'est combien pour la nuit? *say kohnbyahn poor lah nwee*
Can I buy gas?	On peut acheter de l'essence? *ohn puh ashuhtay duh laysohns*
Where is the marina?	Où se trouve le port de plaisance? *oo suh troov luh por duh playzohns*
Can you repair it?	Vous pouvez le réparer? *voo poovay luh raypahray*

WINTER SPORTS

I would like to hire...	Je voudrais louer... *juh voodray looay*
...some skis	...des skis *day skee*
...some ski boots	...des chaussures de ski *day shosewr duh skee*
...some poles	...des bâtons *day batohn*
...a snowboard	...une planche de snowboard *ewn plohnsh duh snowbord*
...a helmet	...un casque *uhn kask*
When does...	À quelle heure... *ah kayl uhr*
...the chair lift start?	...démarre le télésiège? *daymahr luh taylaysyayj*
...the cable car finish?	...ferme le téléphérique? *fairm luh taylayfaireek*
How much is a lift pass?	C'est combien pour le forfait? *say kohnbyahn poor luh fohrfay*
Can I take skiing lessons?	Vous donnez des cours de ski? *voo donay day koor duh skee*
Where are the nursery slopes?	Où sont les pistes vertes? *oo sohn lay peest vairt*

You may hear...

- **Vous êtes débutant?**
  voo zayt daybewtohn
  Are you a beginner?

- **Je dois prendre une caution.**
  juh dwa prohndr ewn kohsyohn
  I need a deposit.

BALL GAMES

I like playing...	J'aime jouer au... *jaym jooey oh*
...football	...football *football*
...tennis	...tennis *taynees*
...golf	...golf *golf*
...badminton	...badminton *badminton*
...squash	...squash *skwash*
...baseball	...baseball *baseball*
Where is...	Où se trouve... *oo suh troov*
...the tennis court?	...le cours de tennis ? *luh koor duh taynees*
...the golf course?	...le terrain de golf ? *luh tairahn duh golf*
...the sports centre?	...le complexe sportif ? *luh kohnplayx sporteef*

le ballon de football
luh balohn duh football
football

les poignets éponge
lay pwannay aypohnj
wristbands

le panier de basket
luh panyay duh basket
basket

le gant de baseball
luh gohn duh baseball
baseball mitt

Can I book a court...	Je peux louer un cours... *juh puh looay uhn koor*
...for two hours?	...pour deux heures? *poor duh zuhr*
...at three o'clock?	...à trois heures? *ah trwa zuhr*
What shoes are allowed?	Faut-il des chaussures spéciales? *fohteel day shosewr spaysyahl*
Can I hire...	Je peux louer... *juh puh looay*
...a tennis racquet?	...une raquette de tennis? *ewn rahket duh taynees*
...some balls?	...des balles? *day bahl*
...a set of clubs?	...des clubs? *day club*
When is the game/match?	À quelle heure est la partie/le match? *ah kayl uhr ay lah partee/luh match*

la raquette de tennis
lah rahket duh taynees
tennis racquet

les balles de tennis
lay bahl duh taynees
tennis balls

la balle de golf, le té de golf
lah bahl duh golf luh tay duh golf
golf ball and tee

le club de golf
luh club duh golf
golf club

GOING OUT

Where is...	Où se trouve... *oo suh troov*
...the opera house?	...l'opéra? *lopairah*
...a jazz club?	...un club de jazz? *uhn klub duh jazz*
Do I have to book in advance?	Il faut réserver à l'avance? *eel foh rayzairvay ah lahvohns*
I'd like...tickets	Je voudrais...billets *juh voodray...beeyay*
I'd like seats...	Je voudrais des places... *juh voodray day plass*
...at the back	...à l'arrière *ah lahryair*
...at the front	...devant *duhvohn*
...in the middle	...au milieu *oh meelyuh*
...in the gallery	...au balcon *oh bahlkohn*
Is there live music?	Il y a un orchestre? *eeleeya uhn ohrkaystruh*
Can we go dancing?	On peut aller danser? *ohn puh allay dohnsay*

You may hear...

- Veuillez éteindre votre portable.
  vuhyay aytahndr votr portahbl
  Turn off your mobile.

- Veuillez retourner à vos places.
  vuhyay ruhtoornay ah vo plass
  Return to your seats.

le théâtre
luh tayahtr
theatre

l'opéra
lopairah
opera house

le musicien
luh mewzeesyahn
musician

le pianiste
luh pyaneest
pianist

le chanteur
luh shohntuhr
singer

le ballet
luh balay
ballet

le cinéma
luh seenaymah
cinema

les popcorns
lay popkorn
popcorn

le casino
luh kahzeeno
casino

la boîte de nuit
lah bwat duh nwee
nightclub

GALLERIES AND MUSEUMS

What are the opening hours?	Quelles sont les horaires d'ouverture ? *kayl sohn lay zohrair doovairtewr*
Are there guided tours in English?	Il y a des visites guidées en anglais ? *eeleeya day veezeet geeday ohn ohnglay*
When does the tour leave?	À quelle heure part la visite? *ah kayl uhr par lah veezeet*
How much does it cost?	C'est combien ? *say kohnbyahn*
How long does it take?	Ça prend combien de temps? *sah prohn kohnbyahn duh tohn*
Do you have an audio guide?	Vous avez un guide audio ? *voo zavay uhn geed audio*
Do you have a guidebook in English?	Vous avez un guide en anglais ? *voo zavay uhn geed ohn ohnglay*
Is (flash) photography allowed?	On peut prendre des photos (au flash)? *ohn puh prohndr day foto oh flash*

la statue
lah stahtew
statue

le buste
luh bewst
bust

Can you direct me to…?	Vous pouvez m'indiquer…? *voo poovay mahndeekay*
I'd really like to see…	J'aimerais beaucoup voir… *jaymuhray bohkoo vwar*
Who painted this?	Qui a peint ça? *kee ah puhn sah*
How old is it?	De quand date-t-il? *duh kohn daht teel*

le tableau
luh tabloh
painting

la gravure
lah gravewr
engraving

le dessin
luh daysahn
drawing

le manuscrit
luh manewskree
manuscript

Are there wheelchair ramps?	Il y a un accès pour les fauteuils roulants? *eeleeya uhn nahksay poor lay fohtuhy roolohn*
Is there a lift?	Il y a un ascenseur? *eeleeya uhn nahsohnsuhr*
Where are the toilets?	Où sont les toilettes? *oo sohn lay twalet*
I'm with a group	Je fais partie d'un groupe *juh fay partee duhn groop*
I've lost my group	J'ai perdu mon groupe *jay pairdew mohn groop*

HOME ENTERTAINMENT

How do I…	Comment fait-on pour… *komohn faytohn poor*
…turn the television on?	…allumer la télévision? *ahlewmay lah taylayveezyohn*
…change channels?	…changer de chaîne? *shohnjay duh shayn*
…turn the volume up?	…monter le son? *mohntay luh sohn*
…turn the volume down?	…baisser le son? *baysay luh sohn*
Do you have satellite TV?	Vous avez la télé satellite? *voo zavay lah taylay sahtayleet*
Where can I buy…	Où peut-on acheter… *oo puh tohn ashuhtay*
…a DVD?	…un DVD? *uhn dayvayday*
…a music CD?	… un CD de musique? *uhn sayday duh mewzeek*
…an audio CD?	… un CD audio? *uhn sayday audio*

le téléviseur grand écran
luh taylayveezuhr grohn taykrohn
widescreen TV

le lecteur de DVD
luh layktuhr duh dayvayday
DVD player

la télécommande
lah taylaykomohnd
remote control

la console de jeux
lah kohnsol duh juh
video game

le baladeur CD
luh baladuhr sayday
personal CD player

l'iPod
leepod
iPod

la radio
lah rahdio
radio

l'ordinateur portable
lordeenatuhr portahbl
laptop

la souris
lah sooree
mouse

Can I use this to…	Je peux l'utiliser pour… *juh puh lewteeleezay poor*
…go online?	…aller sur internet? *allay sewr ahntairnet*
Is it broadband/wifi?	C'est ADSL/wifi? *say ah day ays ayl/weefee*
How do I…	Que faut-il faire pour… *kuh foh teel fair poor*
…log on?	…se connecter? *suh konayktay*
…log out?	…se déconnecter? *suh daykonayktay*
…reboot?	…redémarrer? *ruhdaymahray*

HEALTH

If you are an EU national, you are entitled to free emergency medical treatment in France, but you will have to produce your European Health Insurance Card. It is a good idea to familiarize yourself with a few basic phrases for use in an emergency or in case you need to visit a pharmacy or doctor.

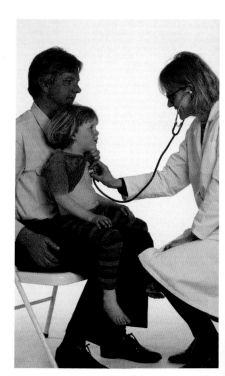

FINDING HELP

I need a doctor	Il faut que je voie un médecin *eel foh kuh juh vwa uhn mayduhsahn*
I would like an appointment…	Je voudrais prendre un rendez-vous… *juh voodray prohndr uhn rohnday voo*
…as soon as possible	…dès que possible *day kuh pohseebl*
…today	…aujourd'hui *oh-joordwee*
It's very urgent	C'est très urgent *say tray zewrjohn*
I have a European Health Insurance Card	J'ai une carte de sécurité sociale européenne *jay ewn kart duh saykewreetay sosyal uhropayen*
I have health insurance	J'ai une assurance maladie *jay ewn assewrohns maladee*
Can I have a receipt?	Je peux avoir un reçu? *juh puh avvwar uhn ruhsew*
Where is the nearest…	Où se trouve la/le plus proche… *oo suh troov lah/luh plew prohsh*
…pharmacy?	…pharmacie? *farmasee*
…doctor's surgery?	…cabinet médical? *kahbeenay maydeekal*
…hospital?	…hôpital? *opeetal*
…dentist?	…dentiste? *dohnteest*
What are the opening times?	Quels sont les horaires d'ouverture? *kayl sohn lay zohrair doovairtewr*

AT THE PHARMACY

What can I take for...?	Qu'est-ce-que je peux prendre pour... *keskuh juh puh prohndr poor*
How much should I take?	Il faut en prendre combien? *eel foh ohn prohndr kohnbyahn*
Is it safe for children?	Les enfants peuvent en prendre? *lay zohnfohn puhv tohn prohndr*
Are there side effects?	Il y a des effets secondaires? *eeleeya day zayfay suhgohndair*
Do you have that...	Vous en avez... *voo zohn navay*
...as tablets?	...en cachets ? *ohn kahshay*
...as a spray	...en vaporisateur ? *ohn vapohreezahtuhr*
...in capsule form?	...en capsules ? *ohn kapsewl*
I'm allergic to...	Je suis allergique au/à la... *juh swee ahlairjeek oh/ah lah*
I'm already taking...	Je prends déjà... *juh prohn dayjah*
Do I need a prescription?	Il me faut une ordonnance? *eel muh foh ewn ordonohns*

You may hear...

- C'est à prendre... fois par jour.
  say tah prohndr... fwa par joor
  Take this...times a day.

- Pendant les repas.
  pohndohn lay ruhpah
  With food.

le bandage
luh bohndaj
bandage

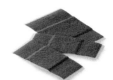

les pansements
lay pohnsmohn
plaster

les capsules
lay kapsewl
capsules

les cachets
lay kashay
pills

l'inhalateur
leenahlahtuhr
inhaler

les suppositoires
lay sewpozeetwar
suppositories

les gouttes
lay goot
drops

le vaporisateur
luh vapohreezahtuhr
spray

la pommade
lah pomad
ointment

le sirop
luh seeroh
syrup

THE HUMAN BODY

I have hurt my…   Je me suis fait mal au/à la…
*juh muh swee fay mal oh/
ah lah*

I have cut my…   Je me suis coupé le/la…
juh muh swee koopay luh/lah

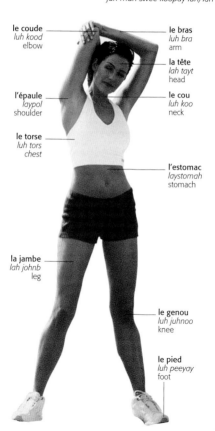

le coude
luh kood
elbow

l'épaule
laypol
shoulder

le torse
luh tors
chest

la jambe
lah johnb
leg

le bras
luh bra
arm

la tête
lah tayt
head

le cou
luh koo
neck

l'estomac
laystomah
stomach

le genou
luh juhnoo
knee

le pied
luh peeyay
foot

FACE

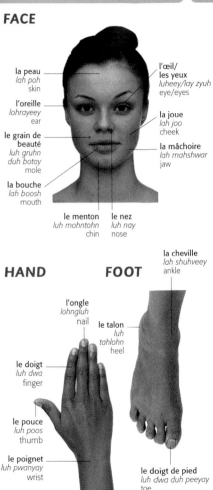

la peau
lah poh
skin

l'oreille
lohrayeey
ear

le grain de beauté
luh gruhn duh botay
mole

la bouche
lah boosh
mouth

l'œil/les yeux
luheey/lay zyuh
eye/eyes

la joue
lah joo
cheek

la mâchoire
lah mahshwar
jaw

le menton
luh mohntohn
chin

le nez
luh nay
nose

HAND

l'ongle
lohngluh
nail

le doigt
luh dwa
finger

le pouce
luh poos
thumb

le poignet
luh pwanyay
wrist

FOOT

la cheville
lah shuhveey
ankle

le talon
luh tahlohn
heel

le doigt de pied
luh dwa duh peeyay
toe

FEELING ILL

I don't feel well	Je ne me sens pas bien *juh nuh muh sohn pah byahn*
I feel ill	Je me sens malade *juh muh sohn malad*
I have...	J'ai... *jay*
...an ear ache	...mal à l'oreille *mal ah lohrayeey*
...a stomach ache	...mal au ventre *mal oh vohntr*
...a sore throat	...mal à la gorge *mal ahla gohrj*
...a temperature	...de la fièvre *duh lah fyayvr*
...hayfever	...le rhume des foins *luh rewm day fwahn*
...constipation	Je suis constipé/constipée *juh swee kohnsteepay*
...diarrhoea	...la diarrhée *lah dyahray*
...toothache	...mal aux dents *mal oh dohn*
I've been stung/ bitten by...	Je me suis fait piquer par... *juh muh swee fay peekay par*
...a bee/wasp	...une abeille/une guêpe *ewn ahbayeey/ewn gayp*
...a jellyfish	...une méduse *ewn maydewz*
...a snake	...un serpent *uhn sairpohn*
I've been bitten by a dog	Je me suis fait mordre par un chien *juh muh swee fay mohrdr par uhn shyahn*

INJURIES

une coupure
ewn koopewr
cut

une égratignure
ewn aygrahteenyewr
graze

un bleu
uhn bluh
bruise

une écharde
ewn ayshard
splinter

un coup de soleil
uhn koo duh solayeey
sunburn

une brûlure
ewn brewlewr
burn

une morsure
ewn morsewr
bite

une piqûre
ewn peekewr
sting

une foulure
ewn foolewr
sprain

une fracture
ewn fraktewr
fracture

AT THE DOCTOR'S

I need to see a doctor	Il faut que je voie un médecin *eel foh kuh juh vwa uhn mayduhsahn*
I'm...	Je... *juh*
...vomiting	...vomis *vohmee*
...bleeding	...saigne *saynyuh*
...feeling faint	...me sens faible *muh sohn faybl*
I'm pregnant	Je suis enceinte *juh swee ohnsahnt*
I'm diabetic	Je suis diabétique *juh swee dyahbayteek*
I'm epileptic	Je suis épileptique *juh swee aypeelaypteek*
I have...	J'ai... *jay*
...arthritis	...de l'arthrite *duh lartreet*
...a heart condition	...un problème cardiaque *uhn problem kahrdyak*
...high blood pressure	...de la tension artérielle *duh lah tohnsyohn artairyayl*

You may hear...

- **Qu'est-ce qui ne va pas?**
  kes kee nuh vah pah
  What's wrong?

- **Où avez-vous mal?**
  oo avay voo mal
  Where does it hurt?

- **Je peux vous examiner?**
  juh puh voo zayxameenay
  Can I examine you?

ILLNESS

le mal de tête
luh mal duh tet
headache

le saignement de nez
luh saynyuhmohn duh nay
nosebleed

la toux
lah too
cough

l'éternuement
laytairnewmohn
sneeze

le rhume
luh rewm
cold

la grippe
lah greep
flu

l'asthme
lassm
asthma

le mal au ventre
luh mal oh vohntr
stomach cramps

la nausée
lah nohzay
nausea

les plaques rouges
lay plak rooj
rash

AT THE HOSPITAL

Can you help me?	Vous pouvez m'aider? *voo poovay mayday*
I need	Je voudrais voir *juh voodray vwar*
...a doctor	... un médecin *uhn mayduhsahn*
...a nurse	...une infirmière *ewn ahnfeermyair*
Where is/are...	Où se trouve/trouvent... *oo se troov/troov*
...the accident and emergency department?	...les urgences? *lay zewrjohns*
...the children's ward?	...le service de pédiatrie? *luh sairvees duh paydyahtree*
...the X-ray department?	...le service de radiologie? *luh sairvees duh rahdyolojee*
...the waiting room?	...la salle d'attente? *lah sahl dahtohnt*

une piqûre
ewn peekewr
injection

un prélèvement de sang
uhn praylaymohn duh sohn
blood test

une radio
ewn rahdyo
X-ray

un scanner
uhn skanair
scan

...the intensive care unit?	...les soins intensifs? *lay swahn ahntohnseef*
...the lift/stairs?	...l'ascenseur/les escaliers? *lasohnsuhr/lay zayskahlyay*
I've broken...	Je me suis cassé... *juh muh swee kahsay*
Do I need...	Il me faut... *eel muh foh*
...an injection?	...une piqûre? *ewn peekewr*
...antibiotics?	...des antibiotiques? *day zohnteebyohteek*
...an operation?	...subir une opération? *sewbeer ewn ohpairahsyohn*
Will it hurt?	Ça va faire mal? *sah vah fair mal*
What are the visiting hours?	Quels sont les horaires de visite? *kel sohn lay zohrair duh veezeet*

un fauteuil roulant
uhn fotuhy roolohn
wheelchair

le bouche à bouche
luh boosh ah boosh
resuscitation

une attelle
ewn atel
splint

un bandage
uhn bohndaj
dressing

EMERGENCIES

In an emergency, you should dial the pan-European number 112 to call an ambulance (*ambulance*), the fire brigade (*les pompiers*), or the police (called *la police* in cities and major towns, but *la gendarmerie* in smaller towns and villages). If you are the victim of a crime or you lose your passport and money, you should report the incident to the police.

IN AN EMERGENCY

Help!	À l'aide ! *ah layd*
Please go away!	Laissez-moi tranquille! *layssay mwa trohnkeel*
Let go!	Lâchez-moi! *lashay mwa*
Stop! Thief!	Arrêtez ! Au voleur! *araytay oh vohluhr*
Call the police!	Appelez la police! *apuhlay lah polees*
Get a doctor!	Appelez un médecin! *apuhlay uhn mayduhsahn*
I need...	Il me faut... *eel muh foh*
...the police	...la police *lah pohlees*
...the fire brigade	...les pompiers *lay pohnpyay*
...an ambulance	...une ambulance *ewn ohnbewlohns*
It's very urgent	C'est très urgent *say tray zewrjohn*
Where is...	Où se trouve... *oo suh troov*
...the British embassy?	...l'ambassade du Royaume-Uni? *lohnbahsahd dew rwahyohm ewnee*
...the British consul?	...le consulat britannique? *luh kohnsewlah breetahneek*
...the police station?	...le commissariat? *luh komeesaryah*
...the hospital?	...l'hôpital? *lopeetal*

ACCIDENTS

I need to make a telephone call	Il faut que je passe un coup de fil *eel foh kuh juh pass uhn koo duh feel*
I'd like to report an accident	Je voudrais faire une déclaration d'accident *juh voodray fair ewn dayklarasyohn dakseedohn*
I've crashed my car	J'ai eu un accident *jay ew uhn akseedohn*
The registration number is...	La plaque d'immatriculation est... *lah plak deematreekewlahsyon ay*
I'm at...	Je suis à... *juh sweezah*
Please come quickly!	Venez vite, s'il vous plaît! *vuhnay veet seel voo play*
Someone's injured	Il y a un blessé *eeleeya uhn blayssay*
Someone's been knocked down	Quelqu'un s'est fait renverser *kelkuhn say fay rohnvairsay*
There's a fire at...	Il y a un incendie à... *eeleeya uhn ahnsohndee ah*
Someone is trapped in the building	Quelqu'un est bloqué dans le bâtiment *kelkuhn ay blohkay dohn luh bateemohn*

You may hear...

- **Quel service désirez-vous?**
  kel servees dayzeeray voo
  Which service do you require?

- **Que s'est-il passé?**
  kuh say teel passay
  What happened?

EMERGENCY SERVICES

l'ambulance
lohnbewlohns
ambulance

les pompiers
lay pohnpay
firefighters

le camion de pompiers
luh kamyohn duh pohnpyay
fire engine

l'alarme incendie
lalarm ahnsohndee
fire alarm

la bouche d'incendie
lah boosh dahnsohndee
hydrant

l'extincteur
lextahnktuhr
fire extinguisher

les menottes
lay muhnot
handcuffs

la voiture de police
lah vwatewr duh polees
police car

le policier
luh poleesyay
policeman

POLICE AND CRIME

I want to report a crime	Je voudrais signaler un délit *juh voodray seenyalay uhn daylee*
I've been robbed	On m'a volé mes affaires *ohn mah volay may zahfair*
I've been attacked	Je me suis fait attaquer *juh muh swee fay atahkay*
I've been mugged	Je me suis fait agresser *juh muh swee fay agresay*
I've been raped	Je me suis fait violer *juh muh swee fay vyohlay*
I've been burgled	Je me suis fait cambrioler *juh muh swee fay kohnbreeyolay*
Someone has stolen…	On m'a volé… *ohn mah volay*
…my car	…ma voiture *mah vvatewr*
…my money	…mon argent *mohn narjohn*
…my traveller's cheques	…mes chèques de voyage *may shek duh vvayaj*
…my passport	…mon passeport *mohn passpor*

You may hear…

- C'est arrivé quand ? *say tareevay kohn* When did it happen?

- Il y a des témoins ? *eeleeya day taymwuhn* Was there a witness?

- Il était comment ? *eel aytay kohmohn* What did he look like?

I'd like to speak to…	Je voudrais parler à… *juh voodray parlay ah*
…a senior officer	…un inspecteur *uhn ahnspayktuhr*
…a policewoman	…une femme policier *uhn fahm poleesyay*
I need…	Je voudrais… *juh voodray*
…a lawyer	…un avocat *uhn navohkah*
…an interpreter	…un interprète *uhn ahntayrprayt*
…to make a phone call	…passer un coup de fil *passay uhn koo duh feel*
Here is…	Voici… *vwassee*
…my driving licence	…mon permis de conduire *mohn pairmee duh kohndweer*
…my insurance	…mes papiers d'assurance *may papyay dasewrohns*
How much is the fine?	À combien est l'amende? *Ah kohnbyahn ay lahmohnd*
Where do I pay it?	Où faut-il payer? *oo foh teel payay*

You may hear…

- **Votre permis, s'il vous plaît.**
  votruh pairmee seel voo play
  Your licence please.

- **Vos papiers, s'il vous plaît.**
  voh papyay seel voo play
  Your papers please.

AT THE GARAGE

Where is the nearest garage?	Où se trouve le garage le plus proche? *oo suh troov luh garaj luh plew prosh*
Can you do repairs?	Vous faites les réparations? *voo fayt lay rayparasyohn*
I need...	Il me faut... *eel muh foh*
...a new tyre	...un nouveau pneu *uhn noovoh pnuh*
...a new exhaust	...un nouveau pot d'échappement *uhn noovoh poh dayshapmohn*
...a new windscreen	...un nouveau pare-brise *uhn noovoh par breez*
...a new bulb	...une nouvelle ampoule *ewn noovel ohnpool*
...new wiper blades	...de nouveaux essuie-glaces *de noovoh zayswee glass*
Do you have one?	Vous en avez? *voo zohn nahvay*
Can you replace this?	Vous pouvez le remplacer? *voo poovay luh rohnplassay*
The...is not working	Le/la...ne fonctionne pas *luh/lah...nuh fohnksyon pah*
There is something wrong with the engine	Il y a un problème au niveau du moteur *eeleeya uhn problaym oh neevoh dew motuhr*
Is it serious?	C'est grave? *say grav*
When will it be ready?	Ça sera prêt quand? *sah suhrah pray kohn*
How much will it cost?	Ça va coûter combien? *sah vah kootay kohnbyahn*

CAR BREAKDOWN

My car has broken down	Ma voiture est en panne *mah vwatewr ayt ohn pahnn*
Can you help me?	Vous pouvez m'aider? *voo poovay mayday*
Please come to…	Vous pouvez venir à… *voo poovay vuhneer ah*
I have a puncture	J'ai un pneu crevé *jay uhn pnuh kruhvay*
Can you change the wheel?	Vous pouvez changer la roue? *voo poovay shohnjay lah roo*
I need a new tyre	Il me faut un nouveau pneu *eel muh foh uhn noovo pnuh*
My car won't start	Ma voiture ne démarre pas *mah vwatewr nuh daymar pah*
The engine is overheating	Le moteur surchauffe *luh mohtuhr sewrshof*
Can you fix it?	Vous pouvez le réparer? *voo poovay luh rayparay*
I've run out of petrol	Je n'ai plus d'essence *juh nay plew daysohns*
Can you tow me to a garage?	Vous pouvez me remorquer jusqu'au garage? *voo poovay muh ruhmohrkay jewskoh garaj*

You may hear…

- **Qu'est-ce qui ne va pas?** *keskee nuh vah pah* What is the problem?

- **Vous avez une roue de secours?** *voo zavay ewn roo duh suhkoor* Do you have a spare tyre?

LOST PROPERTY

I've lost…	J'ai perdu… *jay pairdew*
…my money	…mon argent *mohn nahrjohn*
…my keys	…mes clés *may klay*
…my glasses	…mes lunettes *may lewnet*
My luggage is missing	Mes bagages ont disparu *may bagaj ohn deesparew*
My suitcase has been damaged	Ma valise a été endommagée *mah valees ah aytay ohndomajay*

le portefeuille
luh portuhfuhy
wallet

le porte-monnaie
luh port mohnay
purse

la mallette
lah malet
briefcase

le sac à main
luh sak ah mahn
handbag

la valise
lah valeez
suitcase

le chèque de voyage
luh shayk duh vwayaj
traveller's cheque

la carte de crédit
lah kart duh kraydee
credit card

le passeport
luh passpor
passport

l'appareil photo
laparayeey foto
camera

le téléphone portable
luh taylayfon portabl
mobile phone

I need to phone my insurance company	Il faut que je téléphone à mon assurance *eel foh kuh juh taylayfon ah mohn nassewrohns*
Can I put a stop on my credit cards?	Je peux bloquer mes cartes de crédit? *juh puh blokay may kart duh kraydee*
My name is…	Je m'appelle… *juh mapel*
My policy number is…	Mon numéro d'adhérent est le… *mohn newmairo dadairohn ay luh*
My address is…	Mon adresse est… *mohn nadress ay*
My contact number is…	Mon numéro de téléphone est le… *mohn newmairo duh taylayfohn ay luh*
My email address is…	Mon adresse email est… *mohn nadress email ay*

MENU GUIDE

This guide lists the most common terms you may come across on French menus or when shopping for food. If you can't find an exact phrase, try looking up its component parts.

A

abats offal
abricot apricot
à emporter to take away
agneau lamb
aiguillette de bœuf slices of rump steak
ail garlic
aïoli garlic mayonnaise
à l'ancienne traditional style
à la broche spit roast
à la boulangère baked in the oven with sliced potatoes and onions
à la jardinière with assorted vegetables
à la lyonnaise garnished with onions
à la marinière cooked in white wine
à la normande in cream sauce
à la vapeur steamed
amande almond
amuse-bouche appetizer
ananas pineapple
anchoïade anchovy and tomato paste
anchois anchovies
andouillette spicy sausage
anguille eel
à point medium (steak)
artichaut artichoke
asperge asparagus
assiette anglaise selection of cold meats
au gratin baked in a cream and cheese sauce
au vin blanc in white wine
avocat avocado

B

banane banana
barbue brill (fish)
basilic basil
bavaroise light mousse
béarnaise with butter sauce
bécasse woodcock
béchamel white sauce
beignet fritter, doughnut
betterave beetroot
beurre butter
beurre d'anchois anchovy paste
beurre noir dark, melted butter
bien cuit well done
bière beer
bière à la pression draught beer
bière blonde lager
bière brune bitter beer
bière panachée shandy
bifteck steak
bisque fish soup
blanquette de veau veal stew
bleu very rare
Bleu d'Auvergne blue cheese from Auvergne
bœuf bourguignon casserole of beef cooked in red wine
bœuf braisé braised beef
bœuf en daube beef casserole
bœuf miroton beef and onion stew
bœuf mode beef stew with carrots
bolet boletus (mushroom)

bonne femme traditional "home cooking" style
bouchées small puff pastries
boudin blanc white pudding
boudin noir black pudding
bouillabaisse fish soup
bouilli boiled
bouillon broth
bouillon de légumes vegetable stock
bouillon de poule chicken stock
boulette meatball
bouquet rose prawns
bourride fish soup
brandade cod in cream and garlic
brioche round roll
brochet pike
brochette kebab
brugnon nectarine
brûlot flambéed brandy
brut very dry

C

cabillaud cod
café coffee (black)
café au lait white coffee
café complet continental breakfast
café crème white coffee
café glacé iced coffee
café liégeois iced coffee with cream
caille quail
calamar/calmar squid
calvados apple brandy
canard duck
canard laqué Peking duck
caneton duckling
Cantal white cheese from Auvergne
câpres capers
carbonnade beef cooked in beer
cari curry
carotte carrot
carottes Vichy carrots in butter and parsley
carpe carp

carré d'agneau rack of lamb
carrelet plaice
carte menu
carte des vins wine list
casse-croûte snacks
cassis blackcurrant
cassoulet bean, pork, and duck casserole
céleri/céleri rave celeriac
céleri en branches celery
cèpe cep (mushroom)
cerise cherry
cerises à l'eau de vie cherries in brandy
cervelle brains
chabichou goat's and cow's milk cheese
Chablis dry white wine from Burgundy
champignon mushroom
champignon de Paris white button mushroom
chanterelle chanterelle mushroom
chantilly whipped cream
charcuterie sausages, ham and pâtés; pork products
charlotte dessert with fruit, cream, and biscuits
chasseur with mushrooms and herbs
chausson aux pommes apple turnover
cheval horse
chèvre goat's cheese
chevreuil venison
chicorée endive
chocolat chaud hot chocolate
chocolat glacé iced chocolate
chou cabbage
chou à la crème cream puff
choucroute sauerkraut with sausages and ham
chou-fleur cauliflower
chou rouge red cabbage
choux de Bruxelles Brussels sprouts
cidre cider

citron lemon
citron pressé fresh lemon juice
clafoutis baked batter pudding with fruit
cochon de lait suckling pig
cocotte cooked in a casserole or ramequin
coing quince
colin hake
compote stewed fruit
Comté hard cheese from the Jura
concombre cucumber
confit de canard duck preserved in fat
confit d'oie goose preserved in fat
confiture jam
congre conger eel
consommé clear broth
coq au vin chicken in red wine
coque cockle
coquilles Saint-Jacques scallops in cream sauce
côte de porc pork chop
côtelette chop
cotriade bretonne fish soup from Brittany
coulis sauce or purée
Coulommiers rich, soft cheese
crabe crab
crème cream; creamy sauce or dessert; white (coffee)
crème à la vanille vanilla custard
crème anglaise custard
crème d'asperges cream of asparagus soup
crème de bolets cream of mushroom soup
crème de volaille cream of chicken soup
crème d'huîtres cream of oyster soup
crème pâtissière rich, creamy custard
crème renversée set custard

crème vichyssoise chilled leek and potato soup
crêpe pancake
crêpe de froment wheat pancake
crêpes Suzette pancakes flambéed with orange sauce
crépinette small sausage patty wrapped in fat
cresson cress
crevette grise shrimp
crevette rose prawn
croque-madame grilled cheese and ham sandwich with a fried egg
croque-monsieur grilled cheese and ham sandwich
crottin de Chavignol small goat's cheese
crustacés shellfish
cuisses de grenouille frogs' legs

D

dartois pastry with jam
daurade sea bream
dégustation wine tasting
digestif liqueur
dinde turkey
doux sweet

E

eau minérale gazeuse sparkling mineral water
eau minérale plate still mineral water
échalote shallot
écrevisse freshwater crayfish
endive chicory
en papillote baked in foil or paper
entrecôte rib steak
entrecôte maître d'hôtel steak with butter and parsley
entrée starter
entremets dessert
épaule d'agneau farcie stuffed shoulder of lamb

épinards spinach
**escalope de veau
milanaise** veal escalope
with tomato sauce
escalope panée breaded
escalope
escargot snail
estouffade de bœuf
beef casserole
estragon tarragon

F

faisan pheasant
farci stuffed
fenouil fennel
fève broad bean
filet fillet
filet de bœuf Rossini fillet
of beef with foie gras
filet de perche perch fillet
fine fine brandy
fines herbes mixed herbs
flageolets kidney beans
flan custard tart
foie de veau veal liver
foie gras goose or duck
liver preserve
foies de volaille
chicken livers
fonds d'artichaut
artichoke hearts
fondue bourguignonne
meat fondue
fondue savoyarde cheese
fondue
forestier with mushrooms
fraise strawberry
fraise des bois wild
strawberry
framboise raspberry
frisée curly lettuce
frit deep-fried
frites chips
fromage cheese
fromage blanc fromage
frais
fromage de chèvre
goat's cheese
fruits de mer seafood
fumé smoked

G

galantine rolled, stuffed
meat or poultry
galette round, flat cake or
savoury wholemeal crêpe
garbure thick soup
garni with potatoes
and vegetables
gâteau cake
gaufre wafer; waffle
gelée jelly
Gewürztraminer dry white
wine from Alsace
gibier game
gigot d'agneau leg of lamb
girolle chanterelle
mushroom
glace ice cream
gougère choux pastry dish
goujon gudgeon (fish)
gratin dish baked with
cheese and cream
gratin dauphinois sliced
potatoes baked in cream
gratinée baked onion soup
grillé grilled
grondin gurnard (fish)
groseille rouge redcurrant

H

hachis parmentier
shepherd's pie
hareng mariné marinated
herring
haricots beans
haricots blancs haricot beans
haricots verts green beans
homard lobster
hors-d'œuvre starter
huître oyster

I

îles flottantes soft
meringues on custard
infusion herb tea

J

jambon ham
jambon de Bayonne
smoked and cured ham

julienne soup with chopped vegetables
jus de fruits fruit juice

K

kir white wine with blackcurrant liqueur
kir royal champagne with blackcurrant liqueur
kirsch cherry brandy

L

lait milk
laitue lettuce
langouste spiny lobster
langoustine Dublin Bay prawn/scampi
lapereau young rabbit
lapin rabbit
lapin de garenne wild rabbit
lard bacon
lardon small cube of bacon
légume vegetable
lentilles lentils
lièvre hare
limande lemon sole
Livarot strong, soft cheese
lotte monkfish
loup de mer sea bass

M

macédoine de légumes mixed vegetables
mâche lamb's lettuce
maison home-made
mangue mango
maquereau mackerel
marc grape brandy
marcassin young boar
marchand de vin in red wine sauce
marjolaine marjoram
marron chestnut
massepain marzipan
menthe peppermint
menthe à l'eau mint cordial with water
menu du jour today's menu
menu gastronomique gourmet menu

menu touristique tourist menu
merlan whiting
mesclun dark green leaf salad
millefeuille custard slice
millésime vintage
morille morel (mushroom)
morue cod
moules mussels
moules marinière mussels in white wine
mousseline fish mousse
mousseux sparkling
moutarde mustard
mouton mutton
mulet mullet
Munster strong cheese from eastern France
mûre blackberry
muscade nutmeg
Muscadet dry white wine
myrtille bilberry

N

nature plain
navarin mutton stew with vegetables
navet turnip
noisette hazelnut
noisette d'agneau medallion of lamb
noix nuts, walnuts
nouilles noodles

O

œuf à la coque boiled egg
œuf dur hard-boiled egg
œuf mollet soft-boiled egg
œuf poché poached egg
œufs brouillés scrambled eggs
œuf sur le plat fried egg
oie goose
oignon onion
omelette au naturel plain omelette
omelette paysanne omelette with potatoes and bacon

orange pressée fresh orange juice
oseille sorrel
oursin sea urchin

P

pain bread
pain au chocolat chocolate croissant
pain complet wholemeal bread
pain de seigle rye bread
palette de porc shoulder of pork
palourde clam
pamplemousse grapefruit
pastis anise-flavoured alcoholic drink
pâte brisée shortcrust pastry
pâté de canard duck pâté
pâté de foie de volaille chicken liver pâté
pâte feuilletée puff pastry
pâtes pasta
pêche peach
perdreau young partridge
perdrix partridge
persillade finely chopped parsley and garlic
petite friture whitebait
petit pain roll
petit pois peas
petits fours small pastries
petit salé salted pork
petit suisse fromage frais
pied de porc pig's feet
pigeonneau young pigeon
pignatelle cheese fritter
pignon pine nut
pilaf de mouton rice dish with mutton
pintade guinea fowl
piperade dish of egg, tomatoes, and peppers
pissaladière provençale dish similar to pizza
pissenlit dandelion
pistache pistachio
pistou basil and garlic sauce
plat du jour dish of the day

plateau de fromages cheese board
pochouse fish casserole
poire pear
poireau leek
pois chiches chick peas
poisson fish
poivre pepper
poivron red/green pepper
pomme apple
pomme de terre potato
pommes de terre à l'anglaise boiled potatoes
pommes de terre en robe de chambre/des champs baked potatoes
pommes de terre sautées fried potatoes
pommes frites chips
pommes paille thin chips
pommes vapeur steamed potatoes
porc pork
potage soup
potage bilibi fish and oyster soup
potage Crécy carrot and rice soup
potage cressonnière watercress soup
potage Esaü lentil soup
potage parmentier leek and potato soup
potage printanier vegetable soup
potage Saint-Germain split pea soup
potage velouté creamy soup
potiron pumpkin
pot-au-feu beef and vegetable stew
potée vegetable and meat stew
Pouilly-Fuissé dry white wine from Burgundy
poule au pot chicken and vegetable stew
poulet basquaise chicken with ratatouille

poulet chasseur chicken with mushrooms and white wine
poulet créole chicken in white sauce with rice
poulet fermier free-range chicken
poulet rôti roast chicken
praire clam
printanier with spring vegetables
provençale with tomatoes, garlic and herbs
prune plum
pruneau prune
purée mashed potatoes

Q

quenelle meat or fish dumpling
queue de bœuf oxtail
quiche lorraine egg, bacon, and cream tart

R

raclette Swiss dish of melted cheese
radis radish
ragoût stew
raie skate
raie au beurre noir skate fried in butter
raifort horseradish
raisin grape
râpé grated
rascasse scorpion fish
ratatouille stew of peppers, courgettes, aubergines, and tomatoes
ravigote herb dressing
Reblochon strong cheese from Savoy
rémoulade mayonnaise dressing with herbs, mustard, and capers
Rigotte small goat's cheese from Lyon
rillettes potted pork or goose meat
ris de veau veal sweetbread
riz rice

riz pilaf spicy rice with meat or seafood
rognon kidney
Roquefort blue cheese
rôti roasted/joint of meat
rouget mullet
rouille fish and chili sauce

S

sabayon zabaglione
sablé shortbread
saignant rare
saint-honoré cream puff cake
Saint-marcellin goat's cheese
salade composée mixed salad
salade russe diced vegetables in mayonnaise
salade verte green salad
salmis game stew
salsifis oyster plant, salsify
sanglier wild boar
sauce aurore white sauce with tomato purée
sauce béarnaise thick sauce of eggs and butter
sauce blanche white sauce
sauce gribiche dressing with hard-boiled eggs
sauce hollandaise rich sauce of eggs, butter and vinegar
sauce Madère Madeira sauce
sauce matelote wine sauce
sauce Mornay béchamel sauce with cheese
sauce mousseline hollandaise sauce with cream
sauce poulette sauce of mushrooms and egg yolks
sauce ravigote dressing with shallots and herbs
sauce suprême creamy sauce
sauce tartare mayonnaise with herbs and gherkins

sauce veloutée white sauce with egg yolks and cream

sauce vinot wine sauce

saucisse sausage

saucisse de Francfort frankfurter

saucisse de Strasbourg beef sausage

saucisson salami

sauge sage

saumon salmon

saumon fumé smoked salmon

Sauternes sweet white wine

savarin rum baba

sec dry

seiche cuttlefish

sel salt

service (non) compris service (not) included

sole bonne femme sole in wine and mushrooms

sole meunière floured sole fried in butter

soupe soup

soupe au pistou thick vegetable soup with basil

steak au poivre peppered steak

steak frites steak and chips

steak haché minced beef

steak tartare raw minced steak with a raw egg

sucre sugar

suprême de volaille chicken in cream sauce

T

tanche tench (fish)

tapenade Provencal olive and anchovy paste

tarte tart

tarte frangipane almond cream tart

tartelette small tart

tarte Tatin apple tart

tartine bread and butter

tendrons de veau breast of veal

terrine pâté

tête de veau calf's head

thé tea

thé à la menthe mint tea

thé au lait tea with milk

thé citron lemon tea

tian baked Provencal vegetable dish

thon tuna

tomates farcies stuffed tomatoes

tome de Savoie white cheese from Savoy

tournedos round beef steak

tourte covered pie

tourteau type of crab

tripes à la mode de Caen tripe in spicy sauce

truffe truffle

truite au bleu poached trout

truite aux amandes trout with almonds

truite meunière trout in flour and fried in butter

V

Vacherin strong, soft cheese from the Jura

vacherin glacé ice cream meringue

vanille vanilla

veau veal

velouté de tomate cream of tomato soup

vermicelle vermicelli

viande meat

vin wine

vinaigrette French dressing

vin blanc white wine

vin de pays local wine

vin de table table wine

vin rosé rosé wine

vin rouge red wine

volaille poultry

VSOP mature brandy

Y

yaourt yoghurt

DICTIONARY ENGLISH–FRENCH

The gender of a singular French noun is usually shown by the word for "the": **le** (masculine), or **la** (feminine). When **le** or **la** is abbreviated to **l'** before a vowel, the gender is shown by **(m)** or **(f)**. After plural nouns following **les**, it shown by **(m pl)** or **(f pl)**. The singular masculine form of adjectives is given, followed by the singular feminine form.

A

about **à propos de**
accident **l'accident (m)**
accident and emergency department **les urgences (f pl)**
account number **le numéro de compte**
adapter **l'adaptateur (m)**
address **l'adresse (f)**
adult **l'adulte (m)**
aerobics **l'aérobic (f)**
aeroplane **l'avion (m)**
after **après**
airport **l'aéroport (m)**
air stewardess **l'hôtesse de l'air (f)**
airmail **par avion**
afternoon **l'après-midi (m)**
again **encore**
airbag **l'airbag (m)**
air conditioning **la climatisation**
air travel **le voyage en avion**
aisle seat **la place couloir**
all **tout**
allergic **allergique**
almost **presque**
alone **seul/seule**
already **déjà**
ambulance **l'ambulance (f)**
and **et**
ankle **la cheville**
another **un autre/une autre**
answering machine **le répondeur**
antibiotics **les antibiotiques (m pl)**
apartment **l'appartement (m)**
appointment **le rendez-vous**

April **avril**
apron **le tablier**
arm **le bras**
armband **le bracelet**
arrive (verb) **arriver**
arrivals hall **les arrivées (f pl)**
art gallery **la galerie d'art**
arthritis **l'arthrite (f)**
artificial sweetener **l'édulcorant (m)**
as **comme**
asthma **l'asthme (m)**
at **à**
audio guide **le guide audio (m)**
August **août**
Australia **l'Australie (f)**
automatic ticket machine **le guichet automatique**
autumn **l'automne (m)**
awful **horrible**

B

babysitting **la garde d'enfants**
back (body) **le dos**
back (not front of) **derrière**
backpack **le sac à dos**
bad **mal**
bag **le sac**
baggage allowance **le nombre de bagages autorisé**
baggage reclaim **le retrait des bagages**
baker's **la boulangerie**
baking tray **la plaque de cuisson**

balcony le balcon
ball le ballon
ballet le ballet
bandage le bandage
bank la banque
bank account le compte
  en banque
bank manager le banquier
bank holiday le jour férié
bar le bar
baseball le baseball
baseball mitt le gant de
  baseball
basket le panier
basketball le basketball
bath le bain
bathrobe le peignoir
bathroom la salle de bain
battery la batterie
be (verb) être
beach la plage
beach ball le ballon
  de plage
beach towel la serviette
  de plage
beach umbrella le parasol
beautiful beau/belle
bed le lit
bee l'abeille (f)
before avant
beginner le débutant
behind derrière
below en-dessous
belt la ceinture
beside à côté
bicycle le vélo
bidet le bidet
big grand/grande
bikini le bikini
bill l'addition
black noir/noire
blanket la couverture
bleeding le saignement
blender le mixeur
blood le sang
blood pressure la pression
  artérielle
blood test l'analyse
  sanguine (f)
blue bleu/bleue

board, on à bord
boarding pass la carte
  d'embarquement
boarding gate la porte
  d'embarquement
boat le bateau
boat trip le tour en bateau
body le corps
body lotion le lait corps
bonnet (car) le capot
book le livre
book shop la librairie
book (verb) réserver
boot (car) le coffre
boot (footwear) la botte
bottle la bouteille
bottle opener l'ouvre-
  bouteille (m)
bowl le bol
box la boîte
boy le garçon
boyfriend le copain
bracelet le bracelet
breakdown la panne
breakfast le petit-déjeuner
briefcase la malette
British britannique
broken cassé/cassée
bruise le bleu
brush (hair) la brosse
bubblebath le bain
  moussant
bucket le seau
bumper le pare-choc
burgle cambrioler
burn la brûlure
bus le bus
bus station le dépôt
bus stop l'arrêt de bus (m)
business, on pour affaires
business class la classe
  affaires
bust le buste
butcher's la boucherie
buy (verb) acheter
by par

C

cabin la cabine
cable car le téléphérique

café le café
cake le gâteau
calm calme
camera l'appareil photo (m)
camera bag l'étui (m)
camp (verb) camper
campsite le terrain de camping
camping kettle la bouilloire de camping
camping stove le réchaud
can (verb) pouvoir
can la boîte de conserve
can opener l'ouvre-boîte (m)
Canada le Canada
capsule la capsule
car la voiture
car crash l'accident de voiture (m)
car park le parking
car rental la location de voiture
car stereo la radio
caravan la caravane
caravan site le terrain pour caravanes
carry (verb) porter
cash le liquide
cash machine le distributeur
casino le casino
casserole dish la marmite
castle le château
catamaran le catamaran
cathedral la cathédrale
CD le CD
central heating le chauffage central
centre le centre
chair lift le télésiège
change (money) changer
changing room le vestiaire
channel (TV) la chaîne
cheap bon marché
check in l'enregistrement (m)
check out (hotel) les formalités de départ (f pl)
check-out (supermarket) les caisses (f pl)

cheek la joue
cheers! santé!
cheque le chèque
chequebook le chéquier
chest la poitrine
chewing gum le chewing-gum
child l'enfant (m)
children's menu le menu enfants
chin le menton
chopping board la planche à découper
church l'église (f)
cigarette la cigarette
cinema le cinéma
city la ville
clean propre
cleaner la femme de ménage
cleaning brush le balai
close (near) près de
close (verb) fermer
closed fermé/fermée
clothes les vêtements (m pl)
cloudy nuageux
clubbing sortir en boîte
coast la côte
coat le manteau
coat hanger le porte-manteau
colander la passoire
cold (illness) le rhume
cold (adj) froid/froide
colour la couleur
colouring pencil le crayon de couleur
come (verb) venir
compartment le compartiment
compass la boussole
complain porter plainte
computer l'ordinateur (m)
concert le concert
concourse le hall de gare
conditioner l'après-shampooing (m)
constipation la constipation
consul le consul

consulate le consulat
contact number le numéro
à contacter
contents le contenu
coolbox la glacière
corkscrew le tire-bouchon
cot le lit enfants
couchette la couchette
cough la toux
country le pays
courier le coursier
course le cours
cream la crème
credit card la carte de crédit
crime le crime
crockery la vaisselle
cross trainer le cross trainer
cruise la croisière
cufflinks les boutons de
manchette (m pl)
cup la tasse
current le courant
cut la coupure
cutlery les couverts (m pl)
cycling helmet le casque
de vélo

D

damaged endommagé/
endommagée
dancing danser
dashboard le tableau
de bord
daughter la fille
day le jour
December décembre
deck chair le transat
degrees les degrés (m pl)
delay le retard
delayed retardé/retardée
delicatessen la charcuterie
delicious délicieux/
délicieuse
dentist le/la dentiste
deodorant le déodorant
departure board le tableau
des départs
departures hall les départs
(m pl)
deposit la caution

desk le bureau
dessert le dessert
dessertspoon la cuiller à
dessert
detergent le détergent
develop (a film) développer
diabetic diabétique
diarrhoea la diarrhée
diesel le diésel
digital camera l'appareil
photo numérique (m)
dinghy le bateau gonflable
dining car le wagon-
restaurant
dinner le dîner
disabled parking la place
de parking réservée aux
handicapés
disabled person l'handicapé
(m)
dish le plat
dive (verb) plonger
divorced divorcé/divorcée
do (verb) faire
doctor le médecin
doctor's surgery le cabinet
médical
dog le chien
doll la poupée
door la porte
double bed le lit à deux
places
double room la chambre
pour deux personnes
drawing le dessin
dress la robe
drink (verb) boire
drink (noun) la boisson
drive (verb) conduire
driving licence le permis
de conduire
dry sec/sèche
during pendant
dust pan la pelle
dustbin la poubelle
duty-free shop le magasin
hors taxe
DVD player le lecteur
de DVD

E

each **chaque**
early **tôt**
ear **l'oreille (f)**
east **l'est (m)**
eat (verb) **manger**
elbow **le coude**
electric razor **le rasoir électrique**
electrician **l'électricien (m)**
electricity **l'électricité (f)**
email **l'email (m)**
email address **l'adresse email (f)**
embassy **l'ambassade (f)**
emergency services **les services d'urgence (m pl)**
empty **vide**
engine **le moteur**
English **anglais**
engraving **la gravure**
entrance **l'entrée (f)**
entrance ticket **le billet d'entrée**
envelope **l'enveloppe (f)**
epileptic **épileptique**
equipment **l'équipement (m)**
euro **l'euro (m)**
evening **le soir**
evening dress **la robe de soirée**
examine (verb) **examiner**
exchange rate **le taux de change**
exercise bike **le vélo d'appartement**
exhaust (car) **le pot d'échappement**
exit **la sortie**
expensive **cher/chère**
express service **le service rapide**
extension lead **la rallonge**
extra **en plus**
eye **l'œil (m)**

F

face **le visage**
fairground **la fête foraine**

family **la famille**
family room **la chambre familiale**
family ticket **le billet familial**
fan **le ventilateur**
far **loin**
fare **le prix**
fast **vite**
father **le père**
favourite **préféré/préférée**
February **février**
feel (verb) **se sentir**
ferry **le ferry**
film (camera) **la pellicule**
film (cinema) **le film**
find (verb) **trouver**
fine (legal) **l'amende (f)**
finger **le doigt**
finish (verb) **finir**
fire alarm **l'alarme incendie (f)**
fire brigade **les pompiers (m pl)**
fire engine **le camion de pompiers**
fire extinguisher **l'extincteur (m)**
first **premier/première**
fishing **la pêche**
fishmonger **le poissonier**
fix (verb) **réparer**
flash gun **le flash**
flight **le vol**
flight meal **le repas à bord**
flip-flops **les tongs (f pl)**
flippers **les palmes (f pl)**
flu **la grippe**
fly (verb) **prendre l'avion**
food **la nourriture**
foot **le pied**
football **le football**
for **pour**
fork **la fourchette**
form **la fiche**
fracture **la fracture**
France **la France**
free (not occupied) **libre**
free (no charge) **gratuit/gratuite**
French **français**

fresh frais/fraîche
Friday vendredi
fridge-freezer le réfrigérateur/congélateur
friend l'ami/amie (m/f)
from de
front; in front of devant
frying pan la poêle
fuel gauge le réservoir d'essence
full (hotel) complet/complète
full (glass) plein/pleine
furniture shop le magasin de meubles
fuse box la boîte à fusibles

G

gallery (theatre) le balcon
game le jeu; le match
garage le garage
garden le jardin
gas (heating) le gaz
gear stick le levier de vitesses
get (to fetch) aller chercher
get (to obtain) obtenir
gift le cadeau
gift shop le magasin de cadeaux
gift-wrap faire un paquet-cadeau
girl la fille
girlfriend la copine
give (verb) donner
glass le verre
glasses les lunettes (f pl)
gloss brillant/brillante
go (verb) aller
go out (verb) sortir
goggles les lunettes (f pl)
golf le golf
golf ball la balle de golf
golf club le club de golf
golf course le terrain de golf
golf tee le té de golf
good bon/bonne
goodbye au revoir
good evening bonsoir
good night bonne nuit

grater la râpe
graze l'égratignure (f)
Great Britain la Grande-Bretagne
green vert/verte
greengrocer l'épicier (m)
grill pan le gril
group le groupe
guarantee la guarantie
guest l'invité (m)
guide le guide
guidebook le guide
guided tour la visite guidée
gym la gym

H

hair les cheveux (m pl)
hairdryer le sèche-cheveux
half la moitié
hand la main
hand luggage le bagage à main
handbag le sac à main
handle la poignée
happen (verb) se passer
happy heureux/heureuse
harbour le port
hardware shop la quincaillerie
hatchback le hayon
hate (verb) détester
have (verb) avoir
hayfever le rhume des foins
hazard lights les feux de détresse (m pl)
he il
head la tête
headache le mal de tête
head rest l'appui-tête (m)
headlight le phare
health la santé
health insurance l'assurance maladie (f)
hear (verb) entendre
heart condition le problème cardiaque
heater le chauffage
heel le talon
hello salut
helmet le casque

help (verb) **aider**
her **elle**; **son/sa/ses**
high blood pressure la **pression artérielle**
high chair la **chaise haute**
high-speed train le **TGV**
hiking **partir en randonnée**
him **lui**
hire (verb) **louer**
hold (verb) **tenir**
holiday les **vacances (f pl)**
home à la **maison**
horn le **klaxon**
horse riding l'**équitation (f)**
hospital l'**hôpital (m)**
hot **chaud/chaude**
hotel l'**hôtel (m)**
hour l'**heure (f)**
house la **maison**
hovercraft l'**aéroglisseur (m)**
how? **comment?**
how many? **combien?**
humid **humide**
hundred **cent**
husband le **mari**
hydrofoil l'**hydroglisseur (m)**
hydrant la **bouche d'incendie**

I

I (1st person) **je**
ice la **glace**; le **glaçon**
icy **verglacé/verglacée**
ID la **pièce d'identité**
ill **malade**
illness la **maladie**
in **dans**
indoor pool la **piscine couverte**
inhaler l'**inhalateur (m)**
injection la **piqûre**
injure **blesser**
insect repellent le **produit contre les insectes**
insurance l'**assurance (f)**
insurance company la **compagnie d'assurance**
insurance policy la **police d'assurance**

intensive care unit l'**unité de soins intensifs (f)**
interesting **intéressant**
internet café le **cybercafé**
interpreter l'**interprète (m/f)**
inventory l'**inventaire (m)**
iPod l'**iPod (m)**
iron le **fer à repasser**
ironing board la **planche à repasser**
it **il/elle**

J

jacket la **veste**
January **janvier**
jaw la **mâchoire**
jazz club le **club de jazz**
jeans le **jean**
jellyfish la **méduse**
jeweller le **bijoutier**
jewellery les **bijoux (m pl)**
July **juillet**
jumper le **pull**
June **juin**

K

keep (verb) **garder**; **rester**
kettle la **bouilloire**
key la **clé**
keyboard le **clavier**
kilo le **kilo**
kilometre le **kilomètre**
kitchen la **cuisine**
knee le **genou**
knife le **couteau**
knock down **renverser**
know (people) **connaître**
know (a fact) **savoir**

L

lake le **lac**
laptop l'**ordinateur portable (m)**
large **grand/grande**
last **dernier/dernière**
late **tard**; **en retard**
lawyer l'**avocat (m)**
leak la **fuite**
leave (verb) **partir**
left (direction) **gauche**

left luggage la consigne
leg la jambe
lens l'objectif (m)
lifebuoy la bouée de sauvetage
lifeguard le sauveteur
life jacket le gilet de sauvetage
lift l'ascenceur (m)
lift pass le forfait
light léger/légère
light (noun) la lumière
light (verb) allumer
light bulb l'ampoule (f)
lighter le briquet
lighthouse le phare
like (verb) aimer
line la ligne
list la liste
listen (verb) écouter
little petit/petite
lock (verb) fermer à clé
log on (verb) se connecter
log out (verb) se déconnecter
long long/longue
look (verb) regarder
lose (verb) perdre
lost property les objets trouvés (m pl)
love (verb) adorer
luggage les bagages (m pl)
lunch le déjeuner

M

machine la machine
magazine le magazine
make (verb) faire
mallet le maillet
man l'homme (m)
manual le manuel
manuscript le manuscrit
many beaucoup
map la carte; le plan
marina le port de plaisance
market le marché
married marié/mariée
match (sport) le match
match (light) l'allumette (f)
matt mat/mate

mattress le matelas
May mai
meal le repas
mechanic le mécanicien
medicine le médicament
medium moyen/moyenne
memory card la carte mémoire
memory stick la clé USB
menu le menu
message le message
microwave le micro-onde
midday midi
middle le milieu
midnight minuit
mini bar le mini bar
minute la minute
mistake l'erreur (f)
mist le brouillard
mixing bowl le bol mélangeur
mobile phone le téléphone portable
mole (medical) le grain de beauté
Monday lundi
money l'argent (m)
month le mois
monument le monument
mooring le bassin d'amarrage
mop la serpillère
more plus
morning le matin
mother la mère
motorbike la moto
motorway l'autoroute (f)
mountain la montagne
mountain bike le VTT
mouse (computer) la souris
mouth la bouche
mouthwash le bain de bouche
much beaucoup
museum le musée
music la musique
musician le musicien
must (verb) devoir
my mon/ma/mes

N

nail l'ongle (m)
nail scissors les ciseaux à ongles (m pl)
name le nom
napkin la serviette
nausea la nausée
near près de
nearby proche
neck le cou
necklace le collier
need (verb) avoir besoin
newsagent le tabac-presse
newspaper le journal
never jamais
next prochain/prochaine
new nouveau/nouvelle
nice joli/jolie
night la nuit
nightclub la boîte de nuit
no non
north le nord
nose le nez
nosebleed le saignement de nez
not pas
nothing rien
November novembre
number le numéro
number plate la plaque d'immatriculation
nurse l'infirmière (f)
nursery slopes les pistes vertes (f pl)
nuts les noix (f pl)

O

October octobre
of de
often souvent
oil l'huile (f)
ointment la pommade
on sur
one un/une
online en ligne
only seulement
open ouvert/ouverte
open (verb) ouvrir
opening hours les horaires d'ouverture (m pl)

opera l'opéra (m)
opera house l'opéra (m)
operation l'opération (f)
opposite en face de
or ou
orange orange
order l'ordre (m)
other autre
our notre/nos
outdoor pool la piscine découverte
outside dehors
oven le four
oven gloves les gants de cuisine (m pl)
over au-dessus de
owe (verb) devoir

P

package le paquet
pain la douleur
painkiller l'analgésique (m)
painting la peinture
pair la paire
paper le papier
park le parc
parking le parking
parking meter le parc-mètre
passenger le passager
passport le passeport
passport control le contrôle des passeports
pay (verb) payer
pay in (verb) déposer
pedestrian crossing le passage piétons
peeler l'économiseur (m)
pen le stylo
pencil le crayon
people les gens (m pl)
perhaps peut-être
personal CD player le baladeur CD
pet l'animal de compagnie (m)
petrol l'essence (f)
petrol station la station-service
pharmacist le pharmacien
pharmacy la pharmacie

phone card la carte de téléphone
photo album l'album photo (m)
photo frame le cadre
photograph la photo
photography la photo
pianist le pianiste
picnic le pique-nique
picnic hamper le panier de pique-nique
piece le morceau; la part
pill la pilule
pillow l'oreiller (m)
pilot le pilote
PIN le code secret
pink rose
plaster le pansement
plate l'assiette (f)
platform le quai
play (games) jouer
play (theatre) la pièce
playground le terrain de jeux
please s'il vous plaît
pleasure boat le bateau de plaisance
plug la prise
police la police
police car la voiture de police
policeman le policier
police station le commissariat
policewoman la femme policier
policy la police d'assurance
pool la piscine; le bassin
porter le porteur
possible possible
post (verb) poster
post office la poste
postbox la boîte aux lettres
postcard la carte postale
postman le facteur
prefer (verb) préférer
pregnant enceinte
prescription l'ordonnance (f)
price le prix

print (verb) imprimer
print (photo) la photo sur papier
programme le programme
public holiday le jour férié
pump la pompe
puncture crevé/crevée
purse le porte-monnaie
put (verb) mettre

Q, R

quarter le quart
quick vite
radiator le radiateur
radio la radio
railway le chemin de fer
railway station la gare
rain la pluie
rape le viol
rash l'éruption (f)
razor le rasoir
read (verb) lire
ready prêt/prête
really vraiment
reboot (verb) redémarrer
receipt le reçu
reclaim tag l'étiquette (f)
record shop le disquaire
red rouge
reduction la réduction
registration number la plaque d'immatriculation
remote control la télécommande
rent (verb) louer
repair (verb) réparer
report (verb) dénoncer
report (noun) le rapport
reservation la réservation
reserve (verb) réserver
restaurant le restaurant
restaurant car le wagon-restaurant
resuscitation la réanimation
retired retraité/retraitée
return ticket l'aller-retour (m)
rides les manèges (m pl)
right (correct) vrai
right (direction) droite

river la rivière
road la route
rob voler
robbery le vol
roll (of film) la pellicule
roofrack la galerie
room la chambre
room service le service en chambre
round rond/ronde
roundabout le rond-point
rowing machine le rameur
rubbish bin la poubelle

S

safari park le parc safari
safe en sécurité
sailing faire de la voile
saloon car la berline
same même
sand le sable
sandal la sandale
satellite TV la télé satellite
Saturday samedi
saucepan la casserole
saucer la soucoupe
say (verb) dire
scan le scanner
scissors les ciseaux (m pl)
scooter le scooter
season la saison
second (position) deuxième
second (time) la seconde
sea la mer
seat le siège
see (verb) voir
sell (verb) vendre
sell-by date la date de péremption
send (verb) envoyer
senior citizen la personne âgée
separately séparément
September septembre
serious grave
shampoo le shampooing
shaving foam la mousse à raser
she elle

ship le bateau
shirt la chemise
shoe la chaussure
shop le magasin
shopping faire les courses
shopping mall le centre commercial
shorts le short
shoulder l'épaule (f)
shower la douche
shower gel le gel douche
side effect l'effet secondaire (m)
side dish le plat d'accompagnement
side plate la petite assiette
sign (verb) signer
signpost le panneau
singer le chanteur/la chanteuse
single room la chambre individuelle
single ticket l'aller simple (m)
size (clothes) la taille; (shoes) la pointure
ski (verb) skier
ski boot la chaussure de ski
skin la peau
skis les skis (m pl)
skirt la jupe
slice la part
sliproad la voie d'accès
slow lent/lente
small petit/petite
smoke (verb) fumer
smoke alarm le détecteur de fumée
snack l'en-cas (m)
snake le serpent
sneeze (verb) éternuer
snorkel le tuba
snowboard le snowboard
snow (verb) neiger
so donc; si
soap le savon
socks les chaussettes (f pl)
soft toy la peluche
some quelques
somebody quelqu'un

something **quelque chose**
sometimes **quelquefois**
soon **bientôt**
sorry **pardon; désolé**
south **le sud**
souvenir **le souvenir**
spare tyre **la roue de secours**
spatula **la spatule**
speak (verb) **parler**
speciality **la spécialité**
speed limit **la limitation de vitesse**
speedometer **le compteur de vitesse**
splint **l'attelle (f)**
splinter **l'écharde (f)**
spoon **la cuiller**
sport **le sport**
sports centre **le complexe sportif**
sprain **la foulure**
spray **le vaporisateur**
spring **le printemps**
square (in town) **la place**
squash (game) **le squash**
squid **le calamar**
stairs **les escaliers (m pl)**
stamp **le timbre**
start (verb) **commencer**
statue **la statue**
stay (verb) **rester**
steering wheel **le volant**
step machine **le stepper**
sticky tape **le scotch**
still **encore**
stolen **volé/volée**
stomach **l'estomac (m)**
stomach ache **le mal au ventre**
stop (verb) **s'arrêter**
stop (bus) **l'arrêt (m)**
stopcock **l'arrivée d'eau (f)**
storm **la tempête**
straight on **tout droit**
street **la rue**
street map **le plan**
string **la ficelle**
strong **fort/forte**
student **l'étudiant (m)**

student card **la carte d'étudiant**
suit **le costume**
suitcase **la valise**
summer **l'été (m)**
sun **le soleil**
sunburn **le coup de soleil**
sunglasses **les lunettes de soleil (f pl)**
sunhat **le chapeau de paille**
suntan lotion **la crème solaire**
sun lounger **la chaise longue**
Sunday **dimanche**
sunny **ensoleillé/ensoleillée**
sunscreen **l'écran total (m)**
supermarket **le supermarché**
suppositories **les suppositoires (m pl)**
surf (verb) **surfer**
surfboard **la planche de surf**
sweet **sucré/sucrée**
swim (verb) **nager**
swimming pool **la piscine**
swimsuit **le maillot de bain**

T

table **la table**
tablet **le cachet**
tailor **le tailleur**
take (verb) **prendre**
takeaway **à emporter**
taxi **le taxi**
taxi rank **la borne de taxis**
teaspoon **la cuiller à café**
teeth **les dents (f pl)**
telephone **le téléphone**
telephone (verb) **téléphoner**
telephone box **la cabine téléphonique**
television **la télévision**
temperature **la température**
tennis **le tennis**
tennis ball **la balle de tennis**
tennis court **le court de tennis**
tennis racquet **la raquette de tennis**

tent la tente
tent peg le piquet
terminal le terminal
than que
thank (verb) remercier
that que; ce
the le/la/les
theatre le théâtre
their leur/leurs
theme park le parc
  d'attraction
then alors
there is/are il y a
thermostat le thermostat
they ils/elles
thief le voleur
think (verb) penser
this ceci/cela/ce
three trois
throat la gorge
through à travers; par
thumb le pouce
Thursday jeudi
ticket le billet; le ticket
tight serré/serrée
time l'heure (f)
timetable les horaires
  (m pl)
to à
tobacco le tabac
tobacconist le bureau
  de tabac
today aujourd'hui
toe le doigt de pied
toilet les toilettes (f pl)
toll le péage
tomorrow demain
tonight ce soir
too aussi
toothache le mal de dents
toothbrush la brosse
  à dents
toothpaste le dentifrice
torch la lampe torche
tour guide le guide
tourist information office
  l'office du tourisme (m)
tow remorquer
towel la serviette
town la ville

town centre le centre-ville
town hall la mairie
toy le jouet
traffic jam le bouchon
traffic lights les feux (m pl)
traffic policeman l'agent de
  circulation (m)
train le train
trainers les chaussures
  de sport (f pl)
travel (verb) voyager
traveller's cheque le chèque
  de voyage
trip la balade
trolley le chariot
try (verb) essayer
t-shirt le t-shirt
Tuesday mardi
turn (verb) tourner
twin beds les lits
  jumeaux (m pl)
tyre le pneu
tyre pressure la pression
  des pneus

U

umbrella le parapluie
underground railway
  le métro
understand (verb)
  comprendre
United States les États-Unis
unleaded sans plomb
until jusqu'à
up en haut
urgent urgent
us nous
use (verb) utiliser
useful utile
usual habituel/habituelle
usually d'habitude

V

vacancy la place
vacate (verb) vider
vacuum flask la bouteille
  thermos
validate (verb) valider
valuables les objets de
  valeur (m pl)

value la valeur
vegetarian végétarien/
  végétarienne
venetian blind le store
very très
video game le jeu vidéo
view la vue
village le village
vineyard le vignoble
visa le visa
visit (verb) visiter
visiting hours les horaires de
  visite (m pl)
visitor le visiteur

W

wait (verb) attendre
waiting room la salle
  d'attente
waiter le serveur
waitress la serveuse
wake-up call le réveil par
  téléphone
walk (verb) marcher
walking boots
  les chaussures de
  marche (f pl)
wallet le portefeuille
want (verb) vouloir
ward le service
washing machine le
  lave-linge
wasp la guêpe
water l'eau (f)
waterfall la cascade
waterproofs l'imperméable
  (m)
water-skiing le ski nautique
we nous
weather le temps
website le site web
Wednesday mercredi
week la semaine
weekend le week-end
welcome bienvenue
well bien
west l'ouest (m)
wet mouillé/mouillée
weight allowance le poids
  maximum autorisé

what? quoi ?
wheel la roue
wheelchair access l'accès
  handicapés (m)
wheelchair ramp la rampe
  d'accès handicapés
when? quand?
where? où?
which? lequel?
whisk le fouet
white blanc/blanche
who? qui?
why? pourquoi?
widescreen TV le téléviseur
  grand écran
wife l'épouse (f)
wind le vent
windscreen le pare-brise
windscreen wipers
  les essuie-glaces (m pl)
windsurfer le véliplanchiste
windsurfing la planche
  à voile
windy du vent
wine le vin
winter l'hiver (m)
with avec
withdraw (verb) retirer
withdrawal le retrait
without sans
witness (noun) le témoin
woman la femme
work (verb) travailler
wrapping paper le papier-
  cadeau
wrist le poignet
wrist watch la montre
wrong faux/fausse

X, Y, Z

X-ray la radio
yacht le yacht
year l'année (f)
yellow jaune
yes oui
yesterday hier
yoga le yoga
you tu/vous
your ton/ta/tes/votre/vos
zoo le zoo

DICTIONARY FRENCH–ENGLISH

The gender of French nouns is shown by the abbreviations (m) for masculine nouns and (f) for feminine nouns. Where nouns are in the plural, the gender is indicated by the abbreviations (m pl) or (f pl). French adjectives change according to gender and number. Here the singular masculine form is shown first, followed by the singular feminine form.

A

à at; to
abeille (f) bee
accès handicapés (m) wheelchair access
acheter to buy
accident (m) accident
accident de voiture (m) car crash
accoudoir (m) arm rest
addition (f) bill
adorer to love
adresse (f) address
adresse email (f) email address
adulte (m) adult
aérobic (f) aerobics
aéroglisseur (m) hovercraft
aéroport (m) airport
affaires (f pl) business; pour affaires on business
agent de circulation (m) traffic policeman
aide (f) help
aider to help
aimer to like
airbag (m) airbag
alarme incendie (f) fire alarm
album photo (m) photo album
aller to go
aller-retour (m) return ticket
aller simple (m) single ticket
allergique allergic
allumer to light
allumette (f) match
alors then
amende (f) fine (legal)

ambassade (f) embassy
ambulance (f) ambulance
ami (m)/amie (f) friend
ampoule (f) light bulb
amuser; s'amuser to enjoy
analgésique (m) painkiller
analyse sanguine (f) blood test
anglais English
animal de compagnie (m) pet
année (f) year
antibiotiques (m pl) antibiotics
août August
appareil photo (m) camera
appareil photo numérique (m) digital camera
appartement (m) apartment
appui-tête (m) head rest
après after
après-midi (m) afternoon
après-shampooing (m) conditioner
argent (m) money
attendre to wait
arrêt de bus (m) bus stop
arrêter: s'arrêter to stop
arrivée d'eau (f) stopcock
arriver to arrive
arrivées (f pl) arrivals hall
art (m) art
arthrite (f) arthritis
ascenseur (m) lift
asseoir: s'asseoir to sit
assiette (f) plate
assurance (f) insurance
assurance maladie (f) health insurance

asthme (m) asthma
attelle (f) splint
au-dessus de over
au revoir goodbye
aujourd'hui today
aussi too
Australie (f) Australia
automne (m) autumn
autoroute (f) motorway
autre other
avant before
avec with
avion (m) aeroplane
avocat (m) lawyer
avril April
avoir to have; avoir besoin to need

B

bagage à main (m) hand luggage
bagages (m pl) luggage
bain (m) bath
bain de bouche (m) mouthwash
bain moussant (m) bubblebath
baladeur CD (m) personal CD player
balai (m) cleaning brush
balai d'essuie-glace (m) wiper blade
balcon (m) balcony; gallery
balle de golf (f) golf ball
balle de tennis (f) tennis ball
ballet (m) ballet
ballon de plage (m) beach ball
bandage (m) bandage
banque (f) bank
banquier (m) bank manager
bar (m) bar
barbecue (m) barbecue
barque (f) rowing boat
baseball (m) baseball
bassin (m) pool
bassin d'amarrage (m) mooring
bateau (m) boat
bateau à voile sailing boat

bateau gonflable (m) dinghy
bateau de plaisance (m) pleasure boat
bâtons (m pl) ski poles
batterie (f) battery
beau/belle beautiful
beaucoup many; much
berline (f) saloon car
bidet (m) bidet
bien good; well
bientôt soon
bienvenue welcome
bière (f) beer
bijouterie (f) jeweller's shop
bijoux (m pl) jewellery
bikini (m) bikini
billet (m) ticket
billet d'entrée (m) entrance ticket
billet familiale (m) family ticket
blanc/blanche white
blesser to injure
bleu/bleue blue
boisson (f) drink (noun)
boîte (f) box
boîte de nuit (f) nightclub
boîte de conserve (f) can (noun)
boîte à fusibles (f) fuse box
bol (m) bowl
bol mélangeur (m) mixing bowl
bon/bonne good
bon marché cheap
bonsoir good evening
bonne nuit goodnight
bord, à on board
borne de axis (f) taxi rank
botte (f) boot (footwear)
bouche (f) mouth; bouche d'incendie hydrant
boucherie (f) butcher's
bouchon (m) traffic jam
bouée de sauvetage (f) lifebuoy
bouilloire (f) kettle; bouilloire de camping camping kettle

boulangerie (f) baker's
boussole (f) compass
la bouteille bottle
bouteille thermos (f)
  vacuum flask
la boutique boutique
les boutons de manchette
  (m pl) cufflinks
le bracelet bracelet
le bras arm
brillant/brillante gloss
briquet (m) lighter
britannique British
brosse (f) hair brush
brosse à dents (f)
  toothbrush
brosser to brush
brouillard (m) mist
brûlure (f) burn
bureau (m) desk
bureau de tabac (m)
  tobacconist
bus (m) bus
buste (m) bust

C

cabine (f) cabin
cabine téléphonique (f)
  telephone box
cabinet médical (m)
  doctor's surgery
cachet (m) tablet
cadeau (m) gift; present
cadre (m) photo frame
café (m) café; coffee
caisses (f pl) check-out
calme calm
cambrioler to burgle
camion de pompiers (m)
  fire engine
camper to camp
Canada (m) Canada
canoë (m) canoe
capsule (f) capsule
caravane (f) caravan
carte (f) map
carte de crédit (f) credit
  card
carte d'embarquement (f)
  boarding pass

carte d'étudiant (f)
  student's card
carte mémoire (f)
  memory card
carte postale (f) postcard
carte de téléphone (f)
  phone card
cascade (f) waterfall
casino (m) casino
casque de vélo (m) cycling
  helmet
cassé/cassée broken
casserole (f) saucepan
ceinture (f) belt
château (m) castle
catamaran (m) catamaran
cathédrale (f) cathedral
caution (f) deposit
CD (m) CD
ce this
ceci this
cela that
cent hundred
centre (m) centre
centre commercial (m)
  shopping mall
centre-ville (m) town centre
chaîne (f) channel (TV)
chaise haute (f) high chair
chaise longue (f) sun
  lounger
chambre (f) room
chambre pour deux
  personnes (f)
  double room
chambre familiale (f)
  family room
changer to change money;
  se changer change clothes
chanteur (m) singer
chanteuse (f) singer
chapeau de paille (m)
  sunhat
chaque each
charcuterie (f) delicatessen
chariot (m) trolley
chaud/chaude hot
chaussettes (f pl) socks
chaussure (f) shoe

chaussures de marche
(f pl) walking boots

chaussures de sport (f pl)
trainers

chemin (m) way

chemin de fer (m) railway

chemise (f) shirt

chèque (m) cheque

chèque de voyage (m)
traveller's cheque

chéquier (m) chequebook

cher/chère expensive

cheveux (m pl) hair

chien (m) dog

cigarette (f) cigarette

cinq five

cinéma (m) cinema

ciseaux (m pl) scissors;

ciseaux à ongles (m pl)
nail scissors

classe affaires (f) business
class

clavier (m) keyboard

clé (f) key

clé USB (f) memory stick

climatisation (f) air
conditioning

club de golf (m) golf club

club de jazz (m) jazz club

code secret (m) PIN
number

coffre (m) boot (car)

collier (m) necklace

combinaison(f) wetsuit

comme as; like

commencer to start

comment? how?

commissariat (m) police
station

compagnie d'assurance (f)
insurance company

compartiment (m)
compartment

complet/complète full
(hotel)

complexe sportif (m) sports
centre

comprendre to understand

compte en banque (m)
bank account

compteur de vitesse (m)
speedometer

concert (m) concert

conduire to drive

connaître to know
(people)

connecter: se connecter
to log on

consigne (f) left luggage

constipation (f) constipation

consul (m) consul

consulat (m) consulate

contenu (m) contents

contrôle des passeports
(m) passport control

copain (m) boyfriend

copine (f) girlfriend

corps (m) body

costume (m) suit

côte (f) coast;
à côté beside

cou (m) neck

couchette (f) couchette

coude (m) elbow

couleur (f) colour

coup de fil (m) phone call

coupe-ongle (m) nail
clipper

coup de soleil (m) sunburn

coupure (f) cut

cours (m) course

court de tennis (m) tennis
court

couteau (m) knife

couverture (f) blanket

crayon (m) pencil

crayon de couleur (m)
colouring pencil

crème (f) cream

crème solaire (f)
suntan lotion

crevé/crevée puncture

crime (m) crime

croisière (f) cruise

cuiller (f) spoon

cuiller à café (f) teaspoon;

cuiller à dessert (f)
dessertspoon

cuisine (f) kitchen

cybercafé (m) internet café

D

dans in
danser dancing
date de péremption (f) sell-by date
de from; of
débutant (m) beginner
décembre December
déconnecter
se déconnecter to log out
degrés degrees
dehors outside
déjà already
déjeuner (m) lunch
délicieux/délicieuse delicious
demain tomorrow
dénoncer to report
dent (f) tooth
dentifrice (f) toothpaste
dentiste (m) dentist
déodorant (m) deodorant
départs (m pl) departure hall
déposer to pay in
dépôt (m) bus station
dernier/dernière last
derrière back (not front of), behind
descendre to get off
désolé/désolée sorry
dessert (m) dessert
dessin (m) drawing
détecteur de fumée (m) smoke alarm
détergent (m) detergent
détester to hate
deux two
deuxième second (position)
devant in front of
développer to develop (a film)
devoir to have to (verb); to owe
diabétique diabetic
diarrhée (f) diarrhoea
diésel (m) diesel
dimanche Sunday
dîner (m) dinner
dire to say; tell

disquaire (m) record shop
distributeur (m) cash machine
divorcé/divorcée divorced
dix ten
doigt (m) finger
doigt de pied (m) toe
donc so
donner to give
dos (m) back (body)
douche (f) shower
douleur (f) pain
douloureux/douloureuse sore
douze twelve
droite right (direction)

E

eau (f) water
écharde (f) splinter
économiseur (m) peeler
écouter to listen
écran total (m) sunscreen
édulcorant (m) artificial sweetener
effet secondaire (m) side effect
église (f) church
égratignure (f) graze
électricien (m) electrician
électricité (f) electricity
elle it/she
email (m) email
emporter to take away
en-cas (m) snack
enchanté/enchantée pleased to meet you
encore again; still
endommagé/endommagée damaged
en-dessous below, beneath
enfant (m) child
en plus extra
enceinte pregnant
enregistrement (m) check in
ensoleillé/ensoleillée sunny
entendre to hear
entrée (f) entrance
enveloppe (f) envelope

envoyer to send
épaule (f) shoulder
épicier (m) grocer
épileptique epileptic
épouse (f) wife
équipement (m) equipment
l'équitation (f) horse riding
erreur (f) error
escaliers (m pl) stairs
essence (f) petrol
essuie-glaces (m pl)
  windscreen wipers
est (m) east
estomac (m) stomach
et and
États-Unis United States
été (m) summer
éteindre to turn off
éternuer to sneeze
étiquette (f) reclaim tag
être to be
étudiant/étudiante student
euro (m) euro
examiner to examine
l'extincteur (m) fire
  extinguisher

F

facteur (m) postman
facturer to charge
faire to do; to make
faire les courses to go
  shopping
faire un paquet-cadeau
  to wrap (a gift)
faire de la voile sailing
faux/fausse false; wrong
famille (f) family
femme (f) woman
femme de ménage (f)
  cleaner
femme policier (f)
  policewoman
fer à repasser (m) iron
fermé (m)/fermée (f)
  closed
fermer to close
fermer à clé to lock
ferry (m) ferry

fête foraine (f) fairground
feux (m pl) traffic lights
feux de détresse (m pl)
  hazard lights
février February
ficelle (f) string
fiche (f) form
fille (f) daughter; girl
film (m) film (cinema)
finir to finish
flash (m) flash gun
football (m) football
forfait (m) lift pass
formalités de départ (f pl)
  check out (of hotel)
fouet (m) whisk
foulure (f) sprain
four (m) oven
fourchette (f) fork
fracture (f) fracture
frais/fraîche fresh
français/française French
froid/froide cold
fuite (f) leak
fumer to smoke

G

galerie (f) roofrack
galerie d'art (f) art gallery
gant de baseball (m)
  baseball glove
gants de cuisine (m pl)
  oven gloves
garage (m) garage
garçon (m) boy
garde d'enfants (f)
  babysitting
garder to keep
gare (f) railway station
gauche left (direction)
gaz (m) gas (heating)
gel douche (m) shower gel
genou (m) knee
gens (m pl) people
gilet de sauvetage (m)
  life jacket
glace (f) ice
glacière (f) coolbox
golf (m) golf
gorge (f) throat

grain de beauté (m) mole (medical)
grand/grande big
Grande-Bretagne (f) Great Britain
gratuit/gratuite free (no charge)
grave serious
gril (m) grill pan
grippe (f) flu
groupe (m) group
guarantie (f) guarantee
guêpe (f) wasp
guichet automatique (m) automatic ticket machine
guide (m) guide; guidebook
guide audio (m) audio guide
gym (f) gym

H, I

habituel/habituelle usual
hall de gare (m) concourse
handicapé (m) disabled person
haut, en up
hayon (m) hatchback
heure (f) hour; time
heureux/heureuse happy
hier yesterday
hiver (m) winter
homme (m) man
hôpital (m) hospital
horaires (m pl) timetable
horaires d'ouverture (m pl) opening hours
horaires de visite (m pl) visiting hours
hôtel (m) hotel
hôtesse de l'air (f) air stewardess
huit eight
humide humid
hydroglisseur (m) hydrofoil
ici here
il he/it
il y a there is
imperméable (m) waterproofs
imprimer to print

infirmière (f) nurse
inhalateur (m) inhaler
intéressant interesting
inventaire (m) inventory
invité (m) guest
iPod (m) iPod

J

jamais never
jambe (f) leg
janvier January
jardin (m) garden
jaune yellow
je I (first person)
jean (m) jeans
jet ski (m) jet ski
jeu (m) game
jeu vidéo (m) video game
jeudi Thursday
joli (m)/jolie (f) nice
joue (f) cheek
jouer to play (games)
jouet (m) toy
jour (m) day
jour férié (m) public holiday
journal (m) newspaper
juillet July
juin June
jupe (f) skirt
jusqu'à until

K, L

kilo (m) kilo
kilomètre (m) kilometre
klaxon (m) horn
là-bas over there
lac (m) lake
lait corps (m) body lotion
lampe torche (f) torch
lave-linge (m) washing machine
lecteur de DVD (m) DVD player
léger/légère light
lent/lente slow
lequel? which?
leur/leurs their
levier de vitesses (m) gear stick
librairie (f) bookshop

libre free (not occupied)
ligne (f) line
  en ligne online
liquide (m) cash
lire to read
liste (f) list
lit (m) bed
lit à deux places (m)
  double bed
lit enfants (m) cot
lits jumeaux (m pl) twin
  beds
livre (m) book
local/locale local
location de voiture (f)
  car rental
loin far
louer to hire; to rent
lui him
lumière (f) light (noun)
lundi Monday
lunettes (f pl) glasses;
  goggles
lunettes de soleil (f pl)
  sunglasses

M

machine (f) machine
mâchoire (f) jaw
magasin (m) shop
magasin de cadeaux (m)
  gift shop
magasin hors taxe (m)
  duty-free shop
magasin de meubles (m)
  furniture shop
magazine (f) magazine
mai May
maillet (m) mallet
maillot de bain (m)
  swimsuit
main (f) hand
mairie (f) town hall
maison (f) house
mal bad
mal de dents (m) toothache
mal de tête (f) headache
mal au ventre (m)
  stomach ache
malade ill

maladie (f) illness
malette (f) briefcase
manèges (m pl) rides
manger to eat
manteau (m) coat
manuel (m) manual
manuscript (m) manuscript
marché (m) market
marcher to walk
mardi Tuesday
marée (f) tide
mari (m) husband
marié/mariée married
marmite (f) casserole dish
mat/mate matt
match (m) game; match
  (sport)
matelas (m) mattress
matin (m) morning
me myself
mécanicien (m) mechanic
médecin (m) doctor
médicaments (m pl)
  medicine
méduse (f) jellyfish
même same
menottes (f pl) handcuffs
menton (m) chin
menu (m) menu
mer (f) sea
mercredi Wednesday
mère (f) mother
mes (m/f pl) my
message (m) message
métro (m) underground
  railway
mettre to put
micro-onde (m) microwave
midi midday
milieu (m) middle
mini bar (m) mini bar
minuit midnight
minute (f) minute
moi me
mois (m) month
moitié (f) half
mon/ma/mes my
monument (m) monument
montagne (f) mountain
montre (f) watch

morceau (m) piece
moteur (m) engine
moto (f) motorbike
mouillé/mouillée wet
mousse à raser (f) shaving foam
moyen/moyenne medium
musée (m) museum
musicien (m) musician
musique (f) music

N

nager to swim
nausée (f) nausea
neiger to snow
neuf nine
nez (m) nose
noir/noire black
nom (m) name
nombre de bagages autorisé (m) baggage allowance
non no
nord (m) north
nos (pl) our
notre (sing) our
nourriture (f) food
nous we
nouveau/nouvelle new
novembre November
nuageux cloudy
nuit (f) night
numéro à contacter (m) contact number
numéro de compte (m) account number

O

objectif (m) lens
objets trouvés (m pl) lost property
objets de valeur (m pl) valuables
obtenir to get; to obtain
octobre October
oeil (m) eye
office du tourisme (m) tourist information office
ongle (m) nail
onze eleven

opéra (m) opera
opération (f) operation
orange (f) orange
ordinateur (m) computer
ordinateur portable (m) laptop
ordonnance (f) prescription
ordre (m) order
oreille (f) ear
oreiller (m) pillow
ou/où? where?
oublier to forget
ouest (m) west
oui yes
ouvert/ouverte open
ouvre-boîte (m) can opener
ouvre-bouteille (m) bottle opener
ouvrir to open

P

pack (m) pack
paire (f) pair
palmes (f pl) flippers
panier (m) basket
panier de pique-nique (m) picnic basket
panne (f) breakdown
panneau (m) signpost
pansement (m) plaster
papier (m) paper
papier-cadeau (m) wrapping paper
papiers d'identité (m pl) identity papers
paquet (m) package; packet; parcel
par by; through
parapluie (m) umbrella
parasol (m) beach umbrella
parc (m) park
parc d'attraction (m) theme park
parc-mètre (m) parking meter
parc safari (m) safari park
pardon sorry
pare-brise (m) windscreen
pare-choc (m) bumper
parking (m) car park

parler to speak; to talk

part (f) piece; slice

partir to depart; to leave

partir en randonnée hiking

pas not

passage piétons (m) pedestrian crossing

passager (m) passenger

passeport (m) passport

passer: se passer to happen

passoire (f) colander

payer to pay

pays (m) country

péage (m) toll

peau (f) skin

pêche (f) fishing

peinture (f) painting

pelle (f) dust pan

pellicule (f) film (camera)

peluche (f) soft toy

pendant during

penser to think

père (m) father

perdre to lose

permis de conduire (m) driving licence

personne âgée (f) senior citizen

petit/petite little

petit-déjeuner (m) breakfast

petite assiette (f) side plate

peut-être perhaps

phare (m) headlight; lighthouse

pharmacie (f) pharmacy

pharmacien (m) pharmacist

photo (f) photograph

photographie au flash (f) flash photography

pianiste (m) pianist

pièce (f) play (theatre)

pièce d'identité (f) ID

pied (m) foot

pilates (m) pilates

pilote (m) pilot

pilule (f) pill

pinceau (m) paint brush

pique-nique (m) picnic

piquet (m) tent peg

piqûre (f) injection

piscine (f) swimming pool

pistes vertes (f pl) nursery slopes

place (f) place; square (in town); vacancy

place couloir (f) aisle seat

place fenêtre (f) window seat

place de parking réservée aux handicapés (f) disabled parking

plage (f) beach

plan (m) map

planche à découper (f) chopping board

planche à repasser (f) ironing board

planche de surf (f) surfboard

planche à voile (f) windsurfing

plaque de cuisson (f) baking tray

plaque d'immatriculation (f) number plate; registration number

plaques rouges (f pl) rash

plat (m) dish

plat d'accompagnement (m) side dish

plein/pleine full

pleuvoir to rain

plonger to dive

plus more

pneu (m) tyre

poêle (f) frying pan

poids maximum autorisé (m) weight allowance

poignée (f) handle

poignet (m) wrist

pointure (f) shoe size

poissonier (m) fishmonger

poitrine (f) chest

police (f) police

police d'assurance (f) insurance policy

policier (m) police officer

pommade (f) ointment

pompe (f) pump
pompiers (m pl) fire brigade
port (m) harbour
port de plaisance (m) marina
porte (f) door; gate
porte d'embarquement (f) boarding gate
portefeuille (m) wallet
porte-manteau (m) coat hanger
porte-monnaie (m) purse
porter to carry
porter plainte to complain
porteur (m) porter
portiere (f) door (of car)
possible possible
poste (f) post office
poster to post
pot d'échappement (m) car exhaust
poubelle (f) dustbin; rubbish bin
pouce (m) thumb
poupée (f) doll
pour for
pour affaires on business
pourquoi? why?
pouvoir to be able to
préféré/préférée favourite
préférer to prefer
premier/première first
prendre to take
prendre l'avion to fly
prendre le train to go by train
prés de near; next to
presque almost
pressé/pressée to be in a hurry
pression artérielle (f) blood pressure
pression des pneux (f) tyre pressure
prêt/prête ready
printemps (m) spring
prise (f) plug
prix (m) fare; price
problème cardiaque (m) heart condition

prochain/prochaine next
proche nearby
produit contre les insectes (m) insect repellent
programme (m) programme
propre clean
prospectus (m) leaflet
pull (m) jumper

Q

quai (m) platform
quand when
quarante forty
quart (m) quarter
quatre four
que that; that
quelque chose something
quelquefois sometimes
quelques some
quelqu'un someone; somebody
quincaillerie (f) hardware shop
quitter to leave
quoi? what?

R

radiateur (m) radiator
radio (f) car stereo; radio; X-ray
rallonge (f) extension lead
rameur (m) rowing machine
rampe d'accès handicapés (f) wheelchair ramp
râpe (f) grater
rapport (m) report (noun)
raquette de tennis (f) tennis racquet
raser: se raser to shave
rasoir (m) razor
rasoir électrique (m) electric razor
réanimation (f) resuscitation
réchaud (m) camping stove
recommander to recommend
reçu (m) receipt
redémarrer to reboot
réduction (f) reduction

réfrigérateur (m) fridge
regarder to look;
  to watch
rein (m) kidney
remercier to thank
remorquer to tow
remplacer to replace
remplir to fill
rendez-vous (m)
  appointment
renverser to knock down
réparer to fix; to mend;
  to repair
repas (m) meal
repas à bord (m) flight meal
répondeur (m) answering
  machine
réservation (f) reservation
réserver to book; reserve
réservoir d'essence (m)
  fuel gauge
restaurant (m) restaurant
rester to keep
retard
  en retard late
retrait (m) withdrawal
  (of money)
retraité/retraitée retired
réveil par téléphone (m)
  wake-up call
rhume (m) cold (illness)
rhume des foins (m)
  hay fever
rien anything; nothing
rivière (f) river
robe (f) dress
robe de soirée (f)
  evening dress
rond/ronde round
rond-point (m)
  roundabout
rose pink
roue (f) wheel
roue de secours (f)
  spare tyre
rouge red
route (f) road

S

sable (m) sand
sac (m) bag
sac fourre-tout (m) holdall
sac à main (m) handbag
saignement (m) bleeding
saignement de nez (m)
  nosebleed
saison (f) season
salle d'attente (f)
  waiting room
salle de bain (f) bathroom
salut hello
samedi Saturday
sandale (f) sandal
sans without
santé! cheers!
santé (f) health
sauveteur (m) lifeguard
savoir to know (a fact)
savon (m) soap
scanner (m) scan
scooter (m) scooter
scotch (m) sticky tape
seau (m) bucket
sec/sèche dry
sèche-cheveux (m)
  hairdryer
seconde (f) second (time)
sécurité, en safe
semaine (f) week
sembler to look
sentir: se sentir to feel
séparément separately
sept seven
septembre September
serpent (m) snake
serpillère (f) mop
serré/serrée tight
serveur (m) waiter
serveuse (f) waitress
service en chambre (m)
  room service
service rapide (m) express
  service
services d'urgence (m pl)
  emergency services
serviette (f) napkin; towel
serviette de plage (f)
  beach towel

servir to serve
seul/seule alone
seulement only
shampooing (m) shampoo
short (m) shorts
si so
siège (m) seat
le siège enfant child seat
signer to sign
site web (m) website
six six
ski nautique (m)
  water-skiing
skier to ski; skiing
skis (m pl) skis
snowboard (m) snowboard
soir (m) evening
soleil (m) sun
sortie (f) exit
sortir to go out
sortir en boîte clubbing
soucoupe (f) saucer
souris (f) mouse (computer)
souvenir (m) souvenir
souvent often
spatule (f) spatula
spécialité (f) speciality
sport (m) sport
sports aquatiques (m pl)
  watersports
station de métro (f)
  underground station
station-service (f) petrol
  station
statue (f) statue
store (m) Venetian blind
stylo (m) pen
sucré/sucrée sweet
sud (m) south
supermarché (m)
  supermarket
suppositoires (m pl)
  suppositories
sur on
surfer to surf

T

tabac (m) tobacco
tabac-presse (m)
  newsagent

table (f) table
tableau (m) board
tableau des départs (m)
  departure board
tablier (m) apron
taille (f) clothes size
tailleur (m) tailor
talon (m) heel
tard late
tarte (f) tart
tasse (f) cup
taux de change (m)
  exchange rate
taxi (m) taxi
télé satellite (f) satellite TV
télécommande (f) remote
  control
téléphérique (m) cable car
téléphone (m) telephone
téléphone portable (m)
  mobile phone
téléphoner to phone
télésiège (m) chair lift
téléviseur grand écran (m)
  widescreen TV
télévision (f) television
tempête (f) storm
température (f) temperature
temps (m) weather
tenir to hold
tennis (m) tennis
tente (f) tent
terminal (m) terminal
terminé/terminée finished
terrain de camping (m)
  campsite
terrain pour caravanes (m)
  caravan site
terrain de golf (m)
  golf course
terrain de jeux (m)
  playground
tête (f) head
TGV (m) high-speed train
théâtre (m) theatre
thermostat (m) thermostat
ticket (m) ticket
timbre (m) stamp
tire-bouchon (m) corkscrew
toi you

toilettes (f pl) toilets
ton/ta/tes your
tongs (f pl) flip-flops
tôt early
tour (m) tour
tour en bateau (m)
boat trip
touriste (m) tourist
tourner to turn
tout all
toux (f) cough
train (m) train
transat (m) deck chair
travailler to work
travers, à through
traversée (f) crossing
traverser to cross
trente thirty
trois three
trouver to find
tu you
tuba (m) snorkel ·

U

un/une one
unité de soins intensifs (f)
intensive care unit
urgences (f pl) accident and
emergency department
urgent urgent
utile useful
utiliser to use

V

vacances (f pl) holiday
vaisselle (f) crockery
valeur (f) value
valider to validate
valise (f) suitcase
vapeur, à la steamed
vaporisateur (m) spray
végétarien/végétarienne
vegetarian
véhicule (m) vehicle
vélo (m) bicycle
vélo d'appartement (m)
exercise bike
vélo de ville (m) road bike
vendredi Friday
venir to come

vent (m) wind
du vent windy
ventilateur (m) fan
verglacé/verglacée icy
verre (m) glass
vert/verte green
veste (f) jacket
vestiaire (m) changing room
vêtements (m pl) clothes
viande (f) meat
vider to vacate
vignoble (m) vineyard
vin (m) wine
vingt twenty
viol (m) rape
visa (m) visa
visage (m) face
visite guidée (f) guided
tour
visiteur (m) visitor
vite fast; quick
vide empty
village (m) village
ville (f) city; town
voie d'accès (f) sliproad
voiture (f) car
vol (m) robbery
volant (m) steering
wheel
volé/volée stolen
voler to rob
vos your
vous you
votre your (pl)
vouloir to want
voyage (m) trip
voyager to travel
vrai right (correct)
vraiment really
VTT (m) mountain bike
vue (f) view

W, Y, Z

wagon-restaurant (m)
dining car
week-end (m) weekend
yacht (m) yacht
yoga (m) yoga
zoo (m) zoo

NUMBERS

1 un/une *uhn/ewn*	9 neuf *nuhf*	17 dix-sept *deesayt*	70 soixante-dix *swasohnt-dees*
2 deux *duh*	10 dix *dees*	18 dix-huit *deezweet*	80 quatre-vingts *katruh-vahn*
3 trois *trwa*	11 onze *ohnz*	19 dix-neuf *deesnuhf*	90 quatre-vingt-dix *katruh-vahn-dees*
4 quatre *katruh*	12 douze *dooz*	20 vingt *vahn*	100 cent *sohn*
5 cinq *sahnk*	13 treize *trayz*	30 trente *trohnt*	500 cinq cents *sahnk sohn*
6 six *sees*	14 quartorze *katorz*	40 quarante *karohnt*	1,000 mille *meel*
7 sept *sayt*	15 quinze *kahnz*	50 cinquante *sahnkohnt*	10,000 dix mille *dee meel*
8 huit *weet*	16 seize *sayz*	60 soixante *swasohnt*	

ORDINAL NUMBERS

first premier/ première *pruhmyay/ pruhmyair*	fourth quatrième *katreeyaym*	seventh septième *saytyaym*	tenth dixième *deezyaym*
second deuxième *duhzyaym*	fifth cinquième *sahnkyaym*	eighth huitième *weetyaym*	twentieth vingtième *vahntyaym*
third troisième *trwazyaym*	sixth sixième *seezyaym*	ninth neuvième *nuhvyaym*	

PICTURE CREDITS